i like the idea that
complete strangers
will ~~to~~ be reading
my lists.

mmm...

MA20M

Also by Sasha Cagen

QUIRKYALONE

A Manifesto for Uncompromising Romantics

<u>To Do</u> – <u>March 2001</u>

- get car headlamp fixed
- type Oma's story about posi-
  as Vera for pass in WWII
- pull up clover in garden
- do toxes
- call cat psychic
- clean closet #1
- bring clothes to Goodwill
- clean Hannibal
- mop hall

to-do LIST

FROM **buying milk** TO FINDING A **soul mate**,
WHAT OUR LISTS REVEAL **about us**

Sasha Cagen

A FIRESIDE BOOK | PUBLISHED BY SIMON & SCHUSTER

new york · london · toronto · sydney

Fireside
A Division of Simon & Schuster, Inc.
1230 Avenue of the Americas
New York, NY 10020

First Fireside trade paperback edition November 2007

FIRESIDE and colophon are registered trademarks of Simon & Schuster, Inc.

For information about special discounts for bulk purchases, please contact Simon & Schuster Special Sales at 1-800-456-6798 or business@simonandschuster.com

Designed by Sara Cambridge

Manufactured in the United States of America

10 9 8 7 6 5 4 3 2 1

Library of Congress Cataloging-in-Publication Data

Cagen, Sasha.
    To-do list / by Sasha Cagen.
        p.   cm.
    "This book is a collection of 100 real, handwritten to-do lists and the stories behind them. . . . these lists are real. . . . The people who sent them removed them from their diaries, planners, purses, pockets, and junk drawers so we could get a peek. Their lists offer a rare window into their everyday lives. They show us who we really are, in all our idiosyncratic glory, as opposed to the finished product of ourselves that we reveal to the world"—Introd.
    1. Time management. 2. Self-management (Psychology). 3. Goal (Psychology). 4. Identity (Psychology). 5. Americans—Anecdotes. I. Title.
    HD69.T54C34 2007
    650.1'1—dc22
                                            2006102853

ISBN-13: 978-1-4165-3469-3
ISBN-10:   1-4165-3469-5

For my Mother, Sharon Kernan ...
who taught me that lists are a
way of organizing the universe so
it makes sense, AND who still
leaves lists of things for me to
do when I come home to visit.
Invariably, "unload dishwasher"
tops the list!

INTRODUCTION

What Our Lists Reveal About Us

1 DAILY

Conquering Procrastination • A Frustrated Designer's Pent-up Creativity • Try Not to Go Crazy • Last Day in Mexico Before Going to Japan • A List in Code • Where *Does* the Money Go!? • The List That Won't Die • Potpourri List • Teenage Goals

2 LIFE

Best Friends and Life Plans • Annual Birthday List • To Do Before I Die • Tormented Twenty-Something • His Passion Is That Strong • Lofty Goals • A Thirty-Something Thinks About Going Back to School • Wallowing List • Gutsy Acts • Thirty by Thirty

3 NEW YEAR'S RESOLUTIONS

A Brooklyn Teenage Girl's Resolutions, 1956 • Junior High Self-Improvement • Resolved: Be in the Present Moment • Starting the New Year Right! • Moving to Dubai • A Father's Magic Goals • Just Say Yes 2004

4 DREAM JOBS and bored at work

A Therapist's Fears • Bored at Work • The List Helped in a Perverse Way • Special-Ed Teacher on the Verge • An Art Teacher Who Has Seen Too Many Dead Bears • Contacting God • Behind the Scene of *Freakonomics* • Desert Island Discs • Pros and Cons of a New Job

5 Ideal Mates

ISO a Sock-Darner • A Young Mormon's Ideal Woman • An Eleven-Year-Old Girl's Perfect Husband • Twenty-seven out of Forty-two • Soul-mate Math • Personal Ad Draft • Ready to Meet You • Chubby Is More Preferred • Search Fatigue • Red-State Blue-State Romance • Someone Who Hadn't Yet Existed in My Life

6 Relationships

Next Holiday a Wrapped Present • Workplace Crush • Sleeping on the Couch • Garret Love • A Husband's Ten Steps • Better Off Alone • Topics to Discuss with a Crush • A Soon-to-Be-Divorcée Tries to Move On • Complicated Feelings

"Maybe the creation of lists echoes some distant poetic impulse, the chanting of the names of objects: sun moon stars me you. Perhaps, as in that earliest time, such a calling of things empowers us by momentarily allowing us to order our surrounding world, verbally and symbolically putting everything into a sequence and an arrangement we desire, if only for that instant."

—Robert E. Belknap, *The List: The Uses and Pleasures of Cataloguing*

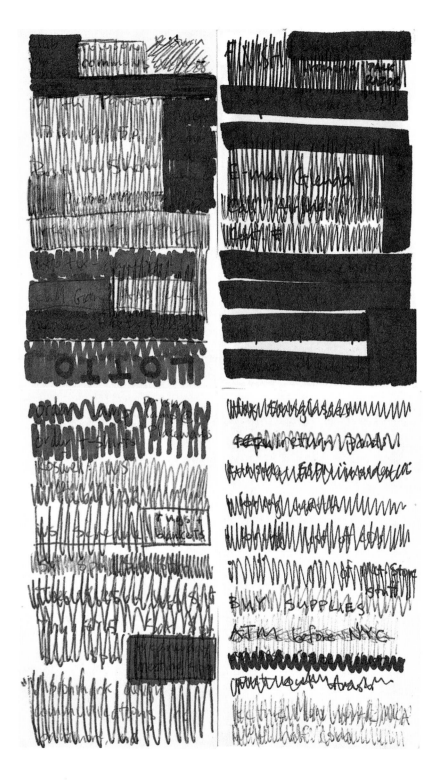

To-do lists on business cards, by Baltimore-based artist Paul Ryan

STATE THEATRE

SUMMER → HAMMONDSPORT ARTS FEST? ~ASFC

LULU.COM   P 3 YRS OF SKETCHBOOK

eMAIL PROFESSORS
→ APPT W/ JOHN!

MARRIAGE LIST &
PERFECT MAN LIST
~WAR MARRIAGE
FROM LIBRARY
TO 88E MKT. APT

CALL ON MONDAY

1 BR & LOFT & PRIVATE entr.
$400+ GAS/ELECTRIC
WATER/TRASH + INCL.
BEFORE 2PM

+ GAS & ELECTRIC
+ INTERNET
+ CELLPHONE

Monday:
Letters: JCrew
Been
BnB

Wed: Post Office
Postcards — Vince
Hanns
Taxes

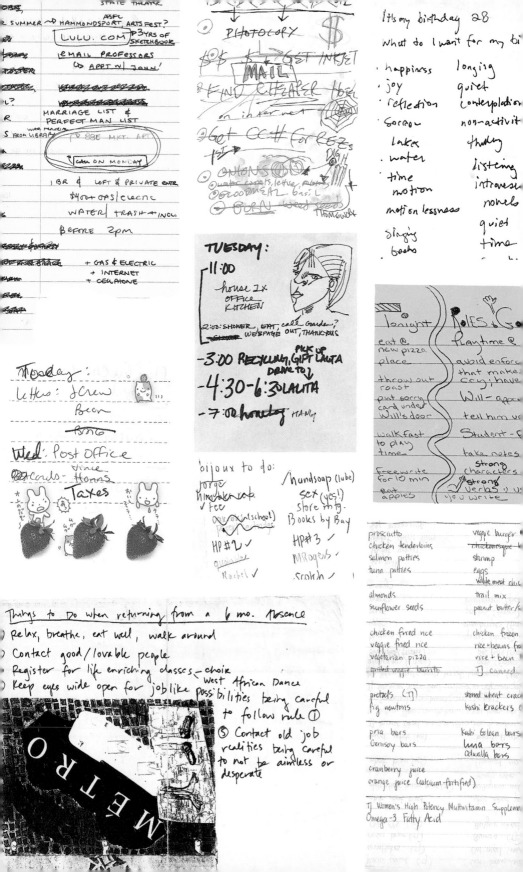

---

① PHOTOCOPY $

$$ → GET INKJET
MAIL
& FIND CHEAPER hotel
on internet

② Got CC# for FEES
$↓
③ ONIONS
water carrots, lettue, potato
④ GOOD MEAL basil
⑤ BURN Weed seeds
THOMGWORK

TUESDAY:
11:00
house 1x
OFFICE
KITCHEN
2:00 SHOWER, EAT, call Garden?
WEBPAGE OUT, THANKYOUS
- 3:00 RECYCLING, PICK UP GIFT LAUTA
DRIVE TO ↓
- 4:30 - 6:30 LAUTA
- 7:00 honey MANG

bijoux to do:
Jorge   / handsoap (lube)
Himalaken cafe   Sex (yes!)
fee   Store mtg.
(in school)   Books by Bay
HP #2 ✓   HP#3 ✓
                       MRogers ✓
Rachel ✓   scotch ✓

Things to Do when returning from a 6 mo. Absence
) Relax, breathe, eat well, walk around
) Contact good/lovable people
) Register for life enriching classes — choir
  West African Dance
) Keep eyes wide open for job like possibilities being careful
     to follow rule ①
  ⑤ Contact old job
    realities being careful
    to not be aimless or
    desperate

METRO

It's my birthday 28
what do I want for my bi

· happiness   longing
· joy   quiet
· reflection   contemplation
· sorrow   non-activity
  lake   thinking
· water   listening
· time   introvert
  motion   novels
  motion lessness quiet
  singing   time
· books

tonight   RULES: G
eat @   Playtime @
new pizza
place   avoid enforce
throw out   that make
roast   cry; have
put sorry   Will — appc
card under
Will's door   tell him v
walk fast   Student - f
to play
time   take notes
freewrite   strong
for 10 min   characters
eat   strong
apples   verbs!! "U
                 you write

---

prosciutto   veggie burger
chicken tenderloins   chicken spare
salmon patties   shrimp
tuna patties   eggs
                          white meat chic

almonds   trail mix
sunflower seeds   peanut butter (TJ)

chicken fried rice   chicken frozen
veggie fried rice   rice + beans fro
vegetarian pizza   rice + bean
grilled veggie burrito   TJ canned

pretzels (TJ)   stoned wheat crack
fig newtons   kashi krackers ✓

pria bars   Kashi Goleen bars
Genisoy bars   luna bars
                          odwalla bars

cranberry juice
orange juice (calcium-fortified)

TJ Women's High Potency Multivitamin Supplem
Omega-3 Fatty Acid

INTRODUCTION

We all know the guilty pleasure of looking in someone's medicine cabinet, refrigerator, or iPod. But what about looking at someone else's to-do list? In a sense, our to-do lists are like diaries, only they're the bullet-point version. Lists can be about anything—from flossing to finding a soul mate, from buying carrots to becoming whole. When we read other people's lists, we uncover the range of meaningful and mundane things that are on their minds. Lifelong hopes and daily tasks mix together, and "organize sock drawer" is on par with "get teaching credential," which is sometimes exactly how life feels.

This book is a collection of one hundred real, handwritten to-do lists and the stories behind them. It's everyday voyeurism, or to put it another way, low-budget reality culture. Unlike what passes for reality on TV, these lists are real. The people who sent them removed them from their diaries, planners, purses, jean pockets, and junk drawers so we could get a peek. Their lists offer a rare window into their everyday lives. They also provide an opportunity for self-examination. Each list is accompanied by a DIY list idea to trigger your imagination and set you down the path of creating your own.

In to-do lists, there are no narratives or artifice, just the essential truth at that one moment—things to do, done, loved, wanted, known. They represent the brain on the page, in its most raw form. They are not only reflections of our mind states, they're also often tools for action and decision making. They represent the conversations that we have with ourselves but don't often voice to others. When we read our own lists ten years later, they can evoke the same emotional states we were in when we wrote them—anxiety, contentment, wistfulness, or hope.

The pleasure of reading other people's lists is certainly voyeuristic, but it's also therapeutic, because there's so much humanity in them. We all wonder, Am I normal? Am I the only one who doesn't have it all figured out? When we only see other people's polished exteriors, it feels like they have some secret that we don't. When we look at other people's lists, we see that functional adulthood doesn't come naturally to everyone else either.

Reading people's lists gives us a unique view into how others motivate themselves to look for love, get to the gym, or quit drinking. We see how they too vow to deal with tasks that are supposed to be natural and elementary, like "pay bills" or "breathe." We see how "get passport" recurs in someone's organizer over several weeks, or that it's not so uncommon to list tasks after we have already accomplished them, simply for the thrill of crossing them off.

Our lists reveal our secret selves. They show us as the hilariously imperfect works-in-progress that we are every single day. We're all figuring it out as we go along, and we're all much funnier, more neurotic, and idiosyncratic than our finished-product versions of ourselves suggest. The evidence is in our lists.

WHERE DID THESE LISTS COME FROM?

Where did this idea come from? The answer, appropriately enough, can be found on another list. Back in 1999, when I was twenty-six and sick of my first job, I decided to start a print magazine about tormented twenty-somethings (and thirty-, forty-, and fifty-somethings who still felt like tormented twenty-somethings) and how they pulled themselves together to become adults—getting a job, a mate, a sense of purpose, a clue. I chose to call it *To-Do List* to express the range of tasks we all need to accomplish to feel like "grown-ups." I placed an ad in another independent magazine asking people to send me their to-do lists in the mail. I really had no idea why or how I would use them. But as soon as lists started to arrive (and from people of all ages) I had a hunch I might be on to something. In those first few months, I would leave work and jog to the post

NOTES
DIARY / IDEAS

SUBJECT: ATM

highway onramp   Games of
Chance

- Weekly Planner
- To·do list
- Face bra
- You jump I jump
- Shoulder pad
- Self-help
- Paperchase
- Control top
- Soft rock
- Adult contemporary
- Master plan
- Strategic Plan
- Power point

Love or career.

Self help book

The hottie list

WWW

Please Understand Me

The Internet

Cursor

32¢ stamp

Username

Search Engine   my

·ga

Choose

Visionquest
Laser tag

Ideas for the name of a new magazine, brainstormed over dinner with
my friend Tara in 1999. Note the second item. Luckily I chose *To-Do List* and not
Face Bra (a device that promises to reverse the signs of facial sagging).

office to get there by closing time. After retrieving the envelopes, I would sit down on the sidewalk to rip them open. The thrill of reading their to-do lists was too great to wait until getting home, or even to a café. At the time, it was hard to pinpoint why reading other people's to-do lists was something I couldn't get enough of. But it felt like I was getting insider information on how other people managed their lives.

Over the last seven years, through *To-Do List* magazine and todolistblog .com, I collected thousands of lists. My apartment could easily be wallpapered with them: daily to-do lists, "Baby Names," "Santa List," "To Do Before I Die," "My Vision of the Perfect Mate," "Places to See, Books to Read," "Things I Like and Hate About My Lover."

I had unwittingly tapped into an unnamed, unexamined community — the listmakers of America (and the world). According to an American Demographics phone survey of one thousand Americans, 42 percent of us make to-do lists. But there are scant studies about us, and obviously still a lot to learn. Who are we and why do we do it? Do we check off or cross off accomplished tasks? Do our to-do lists make us more productive or are they a procrastination tool? Are they part of a belief system that if we are more productive, we're better people?

As you flip through the book, you'll see that many of the lists are relics. Twelve are more than ten years old, and two were written in the 1950s. The degree to which people hold on to lists speaks to their power. It's almost as if they were written on magical, impossible-to-throw-away paper. Some contributors sent me lists that they said they hadn't been able to get rid of for years. They said sending them was cathartic. But then I couldn't get rid of them, out of guilt or a strange sense that the lists had power. A few of them floated around in my backpack until one fell out one day in line at the grocery store, and a shopper behind me said, "Here's your list." I squinted at it. Who's Nick, and why would I need to bring him sheets? Oh yeah, that's someone else's list. Now it's somehow mine.

In editing this collection, I was often stunned by the rawness of the confessions. There might be an element of exhibitionism in publishing a real to-do list, a sense that our lives aren't real unless they have a witness, but there's a generosity in their contributions, too. The lists may be desperate or joyful, but either way they are completely genuine tools that people used in their lives. As Dustin Kidd, whose list "Places Where I Am Stuck Right Now" put it, "I see my list as a little window into my life. I'm proud of the way that I live my life and the way that I make decisions. I hope that sharing the list means sharing a little insight with others who may find some wisdom there."

The lists in this book teach by example. They show us how people use lists to make themselves happier, feel more in control, make decisions, and imagine new mates, jobs, and travel plans. They will also teach you how to be a more creative list-maker. Being exposed to other people's lists definitely increased my repertoire. They also transformed me from a compulsive list-maker addicted to crossing every single thing off to a more imaginative lister who could see the value of throwing wild, even implausible dreams on the page, because who knows?

Lists have always been my natural response to passing depressions and confusion, a reliable way to bring inspiration and order to my life. Just sitting down with a blank page and pen made me feel more in control. But I began to see making lists as a way of life, a way of taking my pulse at any given moment. Lists also became something of an adventure, a mystery, with a feeling of magic attached to them. Items thrown on a list randomly could lead me to unexpected journeys, just like my possible-magazine-names list from 1999 on page 3 led to this book.

I hope this book will take your lists in new directions. The Middle English root of the verb "to list" is "to want" or "to crave"; among other connotations, including our sense of cataloging or grouping, to list once meant to lust, desire, like, or wish to do something. Using the lists in this book as your point of departure, you might articulate desires and dreams you haven't yet voiced. Writing a list can be a secular version of prayer. It's a way of letting the universe know what you want, whether it's a new belt or a new husband. As most list-makers know, writing things down can have a magical way of making them happen.

Opposite: From "100 Things to Do in My Thirties," by Stephanie Debner, 34, Portland, Oregon

32) Be in a performance

33) Take good care of myself,

34) Become friends with an el

35) Become more honest with

36) Go on a silent meditation

37) Do not procrastinate callin

38) Live so that I will have few

39) Develop a real adult relati

90) Hire movers

91) Say no when necessary

92) Remember that I don't alw

93) Let others do things for m

94) Let go of the pursuit of pe

95) Live like the samurai: "To

96) Work on expressing ange

97) Play as much as possible

98) Follow the Golden Rule

99) Being mindful will keep m

100) Grow into a deeper love

"I'M A SLAVE to this LEAF in a DIARY that LISTS WHAT I MUST DO, WHAT I MUST SAY every half hour."

—Israeli Prime Minister GOLDA MEIR, quoted in MS. magazine

1 DAILY

Like many listers, I am disorganized and yet I aspire toward order. My disorganization might be what you call extreme. I hate filing (I basically cannot unless I am jacked up on three cups of coffee) and have never, in my life, balanced a checkbook. I am skeptical of the label, but I will share, for entertainment value, that I have been diagnosed with Executive Deficit Disorder. EDD means, in essence, that the CEO of my brain does not organize information as well as most other people's. I supposedly have problems with managing time and possessions, preparing for short- or long-term assignments, and other skills related to producing work.

According to the doctor who gave me this diagnosis after an hour of ADD testing (what I *thought* I had), there is no cure, except for an organized husband or personal assistant. (Those would be nice.) Initially I was quite upset and called every friend on my cell phone list to discuss.

But here's the thing: Even with my supposed EDD, I manage to get a lot done. Maybe it's a compensating strategy, but my productivity is, I think, much to the credit of my daily lists. Some might call it a dependency, or *strange,* that I write a list a day (and sometimes two or three). I list the smallest things, like "lunch" and the check I'll mail on the way. Perhaps other people float through life doing things in the order in which they occur to them, but for me, there's a perverse process, in which I must first dictate orders to myself.

Daily listers are our own species, really. Non-listers mock us. We amuse them. A woman in a bar tells me that her friends made fun of her when they saw "scrub bathtub" on her list. Why did you have to write that? they asked. But it made perfect sense to me. How could she possibly scrub the bathtub without writing it down first? For me and other daily listers, to-do lists are the way we move through the world. When we write something down, it's five thousand times more likely to happen. They're cheap life coaches, really: free!

Lists help us manage the chaos of ours lives—to impose order, if only for a moment. Writing a list clears the mind. Sometimes it practically feels *cleansing,* to have all the thoughts clamoring for attention find their way to the page. Once everything is written down, it's easier to see which tasks are important and in what order to tackle them. Tasks that seem overwhelming look easier when reduced to mere lines on paper.

who: **A YOUNG JOURNALIST**

age: **23**

date: **THROUGHOUT 1989**

where: **DALLAS**

Conquering Procrastination

"When I wrote this list, I had a tendency to put off tasks that were annoying or unpleasant, and then they would all blob together and become oppressive. Getting them down on paper was the first step toward neutralizing them."

DIY LIST IDEA:
Tasks I've Been Putting Off
(That Will Feel Really Good to Get Done)

Niggling Things to Do

- ✓ Cancel Citibank VISA
- ✓ Straighten out loans
- ✓ Notarize car thing
- ✓ Send AZ query
- ✓ Straighten date book
- ✓ Resolve cat thing
- ✓ Soft-impact aerobics
- ✓ Straighten out bank thing
- ✓ Register to vote
- ✓ Credit card thing
- ✓ Boston U W-2
- ✓ Want
- ✓ diskette thing
- ✓ order courier booklet
- ✓ in-state tuition application
- ✓ state taxes
- ✓ summer registration

who: **MELISSA MARTINS**

age: **25**

date: **NOVEMBER 2004**

where: **SOMERVILLE, MASSACHUSETTS**

A FRUSTRATED DESIGNER'S
PENT-UP CREATIVITY

"I was unemployed, sitting on my living room couch, starting to feel depressed about not getting responses to my résumé. I made this list so I could get all those things that were nagging me onto paper and accomplish them. With a list, these things were all within my control, which I felt I was lacking in my job search. If I couldn't find a job, at least I could fix my oven door!"

> DIY LIST IDEA:
> Illustrate Every Item on a List
> with a Doodle.

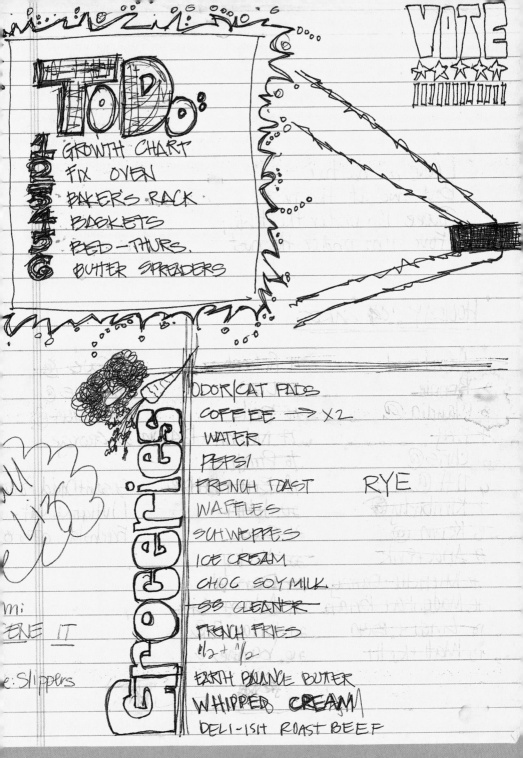

VOTE
★★★★★

To Do:
1. GROWTH CHART
2. FIX OVEN
3. BAKER'S RACK
4. BASKETS
5. BED — THURS.
6. BUTTER SPREADERS

Groceries
- ODOR/CAT PADS
- COFFEE → X2
- WATER
- PEPSI
- FRENCH TOAST   RYE
- WAFFLES
- SCHWEPPES
- ICE CREAM
- CHOC SOY MILK
- SS CLEANER
- FRENCH FRIES
- 1/2 + 1/2
- EARTH BALANCE BUTTER
- WHIPPED CREAM
- DELI-ISH ROAST BEEF

mi
ENE IT

e:slippers

File under: Took more time to make the list than to complete the items on it. —S.C.

who: **NATHAN HARLING**

age: **21**

date: **MAY 2006**

where: **CHICO, CALIFORNIA**

Try Not to Go Crazy

"I made this to-do list for the end of my junior year of college. I realized I had three and a half weeks of work and two weeks to do it. 'Try not to go crazy' was a personal admonishment, since I have a tendency to lose it when overwhelmed. I haven't always made to-do lists. I used to be too prideful to make them, insisting that I don't forget things. It took time for me to wise up and be mature enough to accept my limitations."

DIY LIST IDEA:
Ways to stay sane

financial aid stuff
to "L" practice
walk cycle
read Fong in
Mr. Head
try not to
go crazy

The last item is a laudable goal. —*S.C.*

who: **NATALIA**

for: **HER BOYFRIEND, GUS OSORNO**

age: **17**

date: **JUNE 2005**

where: **ENSENADA, MEXICO**

LAST DAY IN MEXICO
before going to Japan

"My girlfriend wrote this list. It means a lot to me because she wrote it the last day I spent in my hometown, so I wouldn't forget any of my tasks. The next day I left for Japan for a year as an exchange student. When I looked in my back pocket in the Narita airport, the list was there, but I was in a different place. I was so moved I almost started to cry."

DIY LIST IDEA:
If It Were My Last Day at Home
I Would . . .

Guo' "to do" list

* Comer taco fish
* Cenar tacos paisa
* Comer maruchan
* ~~Comer almejas~~
* Comprar Subway
* ~~Ir cartilla~~
* Ir ~~costurera~~
* Recojer ~~copias~~
* Apañar
* ~~Lavar ropa~~
* Ayudar a Natalia a Recojer
* Lavar carro
* ~~Compras d'mama~~
* ~~Lentes~~

TRANSLATION:

Eat fish tacos

Have dinner at Paisa's taco stand

Eat Maruchan (instant cup of noodles)

Eat clams

Buy a Subway (sandwich)

Go get the military service record

Go see the seamstress

Pick up copies

Make out

Do the laundry

Help Natalia clean up her room

Wash the car

Get your mom's stuff

Sunglasses

So they ate clams but didn't make out? Where were their priorities? —S.C.

who: **LISA SHUMICKY**

age: **47**

date: **EASTER NIGHT, 2006**

where: **ISLIP TERRACE, NEW YORK**

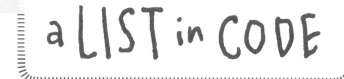

a LIST in CODE

"I wrote this list on Easter night after spending the day with the family at my sister's house. It's (I guess) a list of follow-up things I want to tell or do for my sister:

1. Give her some of the gladiola bulbs from the bag of one hundred I bought at Costco.
2. Suggest that park ranger might be a good career choice for my nephew, who's a high school senior.
3. Send her a thank-you note. '10x' means 'thank you.' I came up with it myself."

DIY LIST IDEA:
Codes I Use on Lists

gladiola melbs

Nora park ranger.

10x

Who would have guessed that "10x" means "thank you"? —*S.C.*

who: **A RECENT COLLEGE GRADUATE**

date: **1989**

where: **DALLAS**

Where DOES the money GO!?

"I was earning money in my first job as a newspaper reporter, so I was giddy with the freedom. But then I'd always wonder why my money disappeared so fast. So I kept the list to see just where fifty dollars went. Frittered away, basically."

DIY LIST IDEA:
Where Did My Last $50 Go?

When does $50 go?

Wed. 6-20	coffee	$1.03
Thu. 6-21	Coke	.50
	wine, etc.	7.46
	Dane's Cut	10.00
Fri. 6-22	gas	11.01
	lunch	4.84
	card for Marc	1.89
	La Madaleine	2.17
	more cards	3.40
Sat. 6-23	garage sale	2.00
	motor oil	3.75

Only $11.01 for gas! (In 1989.) —S.C.

who: **ASHLEY HOFFMAN**

age: **21**

date: **2004**

where: **EUGENE, OREGON**

the LIST that won't DIE

"I was in a rut of stepping into record stores and immediately forgetting what I wanted. This list was to be my cure. This incarnation rode in the back pocket of my jeans for probably eighteen months. It narrowly avoided the wash, but had to be rewritten a few times because of the paper wearing so thin. I only bought one album, *Hockey Night,* which ended up being so great that I bought little else."

DIY LIST IDEA:
Music to Check Out

the high dials

crooked fingers

baby teeth

Acid House Kings

Salteens

The Oggs

~~Ooogggggggg~~

Metric

Ed Herea

Tilly and the Wall

Which lasted longer—the list or these bands? —S.C.

who: **REBECCA STEVENS**

age: **HER EARLY TWENTIES**

date: **CIRCA 1997**

where: **BERKELEY, CALIFORNIA**

POTPOURRI LIST

"What's freaky is how much these ten-year-old lists look exactly like the ones I make now, like I always need toilet paper."

DIY LIST IDEA:
Random Things to Buy

- ~~wash blue for~~
- lil socks, ~~slide on~~ ~~tenzers~~ + barettes
- ~~mail~~ ~~HRP~~ package - *also* packing tape + stamps
- ~~get diamond barette from Mary~~
- get car washed
- ~~work on checkbook~~
- ~~sell clothes @ Crossroads~~
- ~~re-calibrate sewing machine~~
- ~~go through paperwork~~
- ~~shower shit and shave~~
- contact paper
- ~~hole punch~~
- re-write or find "the list"
- ~~spong~~
- ~~clean shower floor~~
- ~~straighten out YMCA~~
- ~~Flk Nurse Betty + return~~
- borrow/buy hor douvre cookbooks
- panties + bras
- ~~2 new prs shoes~~
- ~~drugstore flip flops~~
- ~~insoles~~ 38-5 OF L7
- ~~toilet paper~~
- ~~sex worker romance book~~

who: **KAYLA MURPHY**

age: **17**

date: **AUGUST 2006**

where: **HEMLOCK, MICHIGAN**

teenage goals

"It was summertime when I wrote this list. I wrote it in my bedroom on the floor. I was halfway under my bed. It was neat. I was realizing things—that's all. The X marks are things I finally accomplished. Why did I decide to stop eating pork? I think piggies are cute so I decided to stop eating them. But apparently I don't have enough willpower to turn down a plate of bacon."

DIY LIST IDEA:
Home Improvements to Make

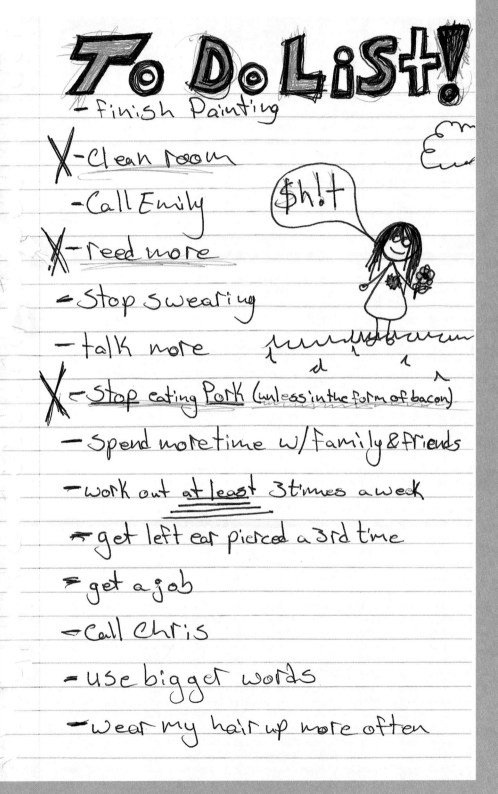

"Living is a constant process of deciding what we are going to do."

—JOSE ORTEGA Y GASSET

2 LIFE

If to-do lists are about the daily grind, life lists are about rising above it. They're not so much about "pick up dry cleaning" or "buy pillow" as they are about "write bestselling novel" and "buy beach house in California" (a lot of people seem to be California dreaming—I wonder if they have any idea how expensive non-beachfront California property is).

To be honest, I haven't really jumped on the life-list bandwagon. I wish I wrote more lists with titles like "To Do Before I Die," but I'm so busy writing to-do lists about returning videos and disputing cell-phone charges. I get very *practical* about my lists, wanting everything to be cross-off-able. I resist life lists, thinking life is such a mystery! I have desires now that I never would have anticipated at twenty-five. How will I know what I want in ten years? What if I don't follow through and disappoint myself? Sitting down to write a life list in the hectic blur of everyday life feels too pressured, too intimidating.

But maybe that's because life lists have a time and a place, and that's often when we are going through a big life transition, on a birthday, or at the very least, at a café. When I do get into the soul-searching, hopeful life-list mentality, it's often when I'm three thousand miles from home, seized by a sense of possibility of how my life could change. I've made lists of things to do in the next ten years—start my own magazine again, this time with funding, travel in South America, own a house with a wraparound porch. It feels liberating to let go of the critical mind that asks us to write only to-dos that are obviously achievable. Who knows, maybe some of those people will own beach houses in California. If they don't, who cares? At least they had the guts to voice their dreams. Living with a sense of possibility is in and of itself rewarding.

People write life lists at all ages. In fact, it's probably even more important for people to write life lists in their fifties or sixties, when we're expected to settle into narrowly defined worlds. But most of these lists were written by people in their twenties and thirties, whose lives hadn't yet settled into predictable patterns, when they were still wondering and worrying about what direction their lives would take. Their lists are often attempts to respond to the question, "What should I do with my life?" It used to be that we all had to follow the same to-do list for life: go to high school, get married, maybe college, have children. Now it's up to us to make our own life plans.

who: **CAMERON TUTTLE, author of the
bestselling _Bad Girl's Guide_ series**

age: **26**

date: **MARCH 12, 1989**

where: **NEW YORK CITY**

best FRIENDS and
LIFE _plans_

"I wrote this list when I was living in New York with my best friend, Dana. We were discussing our life plans and trying to close the gap between our unsatisfying young-career-girl reality and our dreams. My list was actually written by Dana. I was talking and she was writing.

"I was working at an ad agency and suffering. It wasn't a position that demanded much creativity. I really wanted to be a writer, but I couldn't figure out how. And I had trouble finishing things. (See "greeting card" under "job options.") Apparently, I thought writing greeting cards was the perfect solution. Sadly, it looks like I only had one card idea.

"Did I find an apartment to buy by September of that year? No. (I bought my first house sixteen years later!) Did I get healthy? Well, yes and no. I did stop 'dipping' (chewing tobacco). It was a bad habit that I picked up from an old boyfriend. But damn, you sure get a wicked rush.

"I feel both happy and sad looking back on this list. I feel proud that I finally figured out how to be a writer, but I miss the random creativity in my life. And I miss Dana. We haven't spoken in years. But you'll have to ask her about that."

_DIY LIST IDEA:
My Six-Month Life Plan as Written
by My Friend / My Friend's Six-Month
Life Plan as Written by Me_

Cameron's Plan

By September I will have:

- found an apartment to buy (w/ Dana's help)
- Still be at Warwick (but looking on ...)
- ~~Looking on to~~ Finish a screenplay
- get healthy
  - stop picking at skin
  - Stress management
  - exercise - Run nightly 8:00 PM 3/13/89
  - stop dipping
- Create more FUNCTIONAL ART
- Market Photos of "Functional Art"
- Work less = better hours

Job options:
- Free Lance writing for magazines
- Comercials
  - Agent
- find a Writing Agent to market screenplay
- Greeting Card

Future Options (Sept. on)

- GREc => Grad school aps.

A complete plan—from "grad school" to "stop picking at skin." —S.C.

who: **A WOMAN POET**

age: **ON HER FORTIETH BIRTHDAY**

date: **JUNE 24, 2006**

where: **ON A VISIT TO PARIS**

ANNUAL BIRTHDAY LIST

"Years ago, when I lived in New York City, I went through a long period when I didn't know what I was doing with my life, which way to turn with my career, personal life, etc. So I started going to see corner psychics on a whim. Usually I took what they said with a grain of salt and just used the session to gauge my own feelings.

"Someone I worked with told me about a really primo psychic, however, and I decided to splurge and go to her. She probably was the most prescient of all the psychics I ever went to, although I can't really remember if much of what she said came true. But she told me that everyone gets seven wishes on their birthday, and to make them happen you have to write them down. I went to see this psychic just before my thirtieth birthday and have been making a birthday list ever since.

"Have any wishes come true? I think they're starting to. That morning in Paris I got flowers from someone I am now happily dating! I think making the list, every year, is a way of signaling to myself what I want to happen internally, and then in a more mystical sense, bring outward to the world."

DIY LIST IDEA:
Seven Birthday Wishes

32   Sasha Cagen

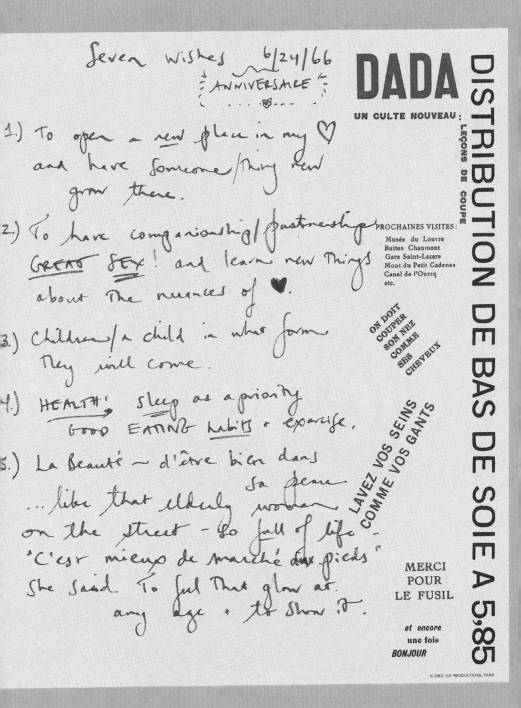

Seven Wishes 6/24/66
ANNIVERSAIRE

1.) To open a *new* place in my ♡
and have someone/thing new
grow there.

2.) To have companionship/partnership
GREAT SEX! and learn new things
about the nuances of ♥.

3.) Children/a child in what form
they will come.

4.) HEALTH! sleep as a priority
GOOD EATING habits + exercise.

5.) La Beauté ~ d'être bien dans
...like that elderly woman sa peau
on the street – so full of life.
"C'est mieux de marché aux pieds"
she said. To feel that glow at
any age + to show it.

DADA

UN CULTE NOUVEAU:

DISTRIBUTION DE BAS DE SOIE A 5.85
LEÇONS DE COUPE

PROCHAINES VISITES:
Musée du Louvre
Buttes Chaumont
Gare Saint-Lazare
Mont du Petit Cadenas
Canal de l'Ourcq
etc.

ON DOIT COUPER SON NEZ COMME SES CHEVEUX

LAVEZ VOS SEINS COMME VOS GANTS

MERCI
POUR
LE FUSIL

et encore
une fois
BONJOUR

© 2005 JNF PRODUCTIONS, PARIS

D'être bien dans sa peau = feeling good in one's skin. —S.C.

(Wishes 6 and 7 on p. 234)

who: **IRENE OUET**

age: **29**

date: **FEBRUARY 2005**

where: **MENDOZA, ARGENTINA**
(on the job at a winery)

To Do Before I Die

"I have a list for everything. My friends call me list girl. Have I done any of these things yet? I have worked as a bartender, and I have KitchenAid products. My most important goal? The blue house in front of the ocean, with a huge kitchen."

DIY LIST IDEA:
If I Got These Things I Would Ask
for Nothing Else

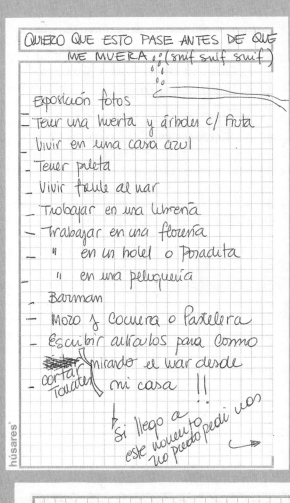

TRANSLATION:

Photo show

Have my own garden with fruit trees

Live in a blue house

Have a swimming pool

Live facing the sea

Work in a bookstore

Work in a flower shop

Work in a lodge or bed-and-breakfast

Work in a salon

Bartender

Waitress and a cook or pastry chef

Write articles for *Cosmo* watching the sea from my house!!

Harvest tomatoes

If I arrive at this moment I would ask for nothing else

Be a proud mother

Have my son be proud of me

Travel around the world

Have a kitchen full of KitchenAid and Viking products

One list, eight careers. Good thing she's only twenty-nine! —*S.C.*

TORMENTED
TWENTY-SOMETHING

"This is a weird list. 'Become whole'? Was I supposed to cross that off? That's done? It looks like I was fairly in touch with myself, but I guess I didn't feel like I was a whole person. I was in turmoil all the way through my early twenties and knew there were things I was starting to figure out. A lot of my lists from this period seem to get weird at the end. They end with some kind of grand finale; another one says 'don't get swallowed up' at the end."

DIY LIST IDEA:
Ways I'm Whole Already

- ALWAYS LEARNING! FORMAL EDUCATION?
- MAKE ACTIVISM/NON-PROFIT MY DAY JOB.
- ART/CREATIVITY AS INTEGRAL PART OF MY LIFE.
- TRAVEL.
- GET LAND.
- TAKE CARE OF MYSELF.
- WORK LESS →→→ GET OUT OF THE SYSTEM.
- BECOME WHOLE.

That's "get *land*," not "get *laid*." —S.C.

who: **JONATHAN FORTE**

age: **NEWLY 25**

date: **JUNE 2006**

where: **AT THE LIBRARY in Merrick,**
New York

his PASSION is that STRONG

"Much has changed since I wrote my list. Since then, I've received a job offer and moved to New Jersey. I currently work as a court interpreter for the New Jersey Judiciary. And I am still beaming at the fact that I now live right next door to my best friend! As for classic films, since age eleven or twelve, I have been enamored of old films. I want to see as many films as I can, preferably on the big screen, because my passion for them is that strong."

DIY LIST IDEA:
Hobbies to Take Up

Jonathan Forte

Things to Do Before I Turn 30
(written June, 2006)

1) See at least 1500 pre-1960 Hollywood movies and read as many books about old Hollywood as I possibly can.

2.) Become a federally-certified court interpreter

3) Keep a daily journal

4.) Live in Latin America for a month or two

5.) Write some articles about Hollywood's Golden Age

6.) Visit San Francisco and attend the Noir City Film Festival

7) Fall in love for the first time

8.) Continue to have great times with my best friend (Most Important) I guess I saved the best for last! :)

who: **LUKE RAYMOND**

age: **20 (revised at 23)**

date: **SUMMER 2003 AND 2006**

where: **ROSEBURG, OREGON**

LOFTY *goals*

"When I wrote this list I was broke, going to school off and on, hated my job, and had just moved in with my parents. My girlfriend was really on me to get my life together. I sat down one day and decided to write down everything I wanted to do in my lifetime. I have a real fear of lying on my deathbed and not being able to say I did anything worthwhile. This list is what came out.

"Three years later I pulled my list out and cleaned it up. I have to admit that I haven't done anything on it other than read. I have read more than a book a month, which makes me happy. Why would I want to throw a hand grenade? I can't really give a good answer, other than that it would be fun. I don't want to hurt anyone, I just think it would be cool to throw one and see and hear it explode.

"I know I'll add more goals. Perhaps one day I'll even want to get married and have children and own a house in a trendy neighborhood. I still feel that traveling is my greatest desire. I've become more realistic and am starting to realize the effort some of these goals will require. For many of these I'll need a career. I'm ready to accept that and work toward that. When I first wrote this list, a career was the last thing I wanted. I still don't feel excited about working forty hours a week for the next forty years, but I guess it's something most Americans are forced to do if they don't want a life of poverty. If I can accomplish these goals it will make up for all the years I'll lose at work."

DIY LIST IDEA:
My Ultimate To-Do List

Ultimate to do list   7-8-2006
(Revised 2003 list)

1. Sky dive
2. Drive an exotic car
3. Buy a motorcycle
4. Restore a car ('69 Camaro)
5. Attend performance driving school
6. Visit every continent
7. Live in a foreign country
8. Become fluent in a foreign language
9. Stay in a rainforest at least 1 week
10. Travel around the world without aid of an airplane
11. Stay on a deserted island (tropical)
12. Be in a working band
13. Build a guitar
14. Cause a big explosion. Preferably planed
15. Scuba dive
16. Explore underwater wreckage
17. Involved in archaeological excavation
18. Drive in a demolition derby
19. Discover something
20. Get what I consider very good at guitar
21. Buy and restore an old house
22. Stay somewhere "haunted"
23. Fire a cannon. (Live shot)
24. Learn to fence
25 Throw a hand gremade
26. Climb a mountain
27. Ride in a hot air balloon

28. Make a time-capsule
29. Get a college degree. (4 year)
30. Break the sound barrier
31. Learn to pick locks
32. Read at least 12 books a year
33. Drive rally-cross
34. Learn to play drums
35. Drive the Autobahn
36. Experience zero-gravity (space)

I'm *hoping* the explosion will be planned. —*S.C.*

who: **ADAM DINGLE**

age: **33**

date: **OCTOBER 2003**

where: **ON A TRAIN, commuting to work**
in Silicon Valley

a THirty-Something thinks about going back to School

"I was thinking about going back to grad school in computer science and decided to brush up on my GRE vocabulary. In making the list a couple of things surprised me. First I was surprised by how many GRE words now seemed obvious to me. My vocabulary had naturally expanded quite a bit since college. (In retrospect that shouldn't be too remarkable. I've heard that vocabulary size is one of few ways in which we all improve continuously until we die.) I was also surprised by how many familiar-sounding words I found myself unable to define with any precision. I've realized there's a large gray zone between not knowing and knowing a word, and lots of GRE words seem to live there. I never ended up taking the GRE. So the list mostly helped me as a source of amusement at a party I hosted four years later: I cut out individual words and gave them to people and challenged them to use them in conversation at the party without being called on it."

DIY LIST IDEA:

Words I Enjoy

sybarite

restive

pusillanimous

~~disgorge~~

blandish

ponderous

afferent

subaltern

apprise

craven

~~freckle~~

contumacious

~~brook~~

refractory

proscribe

occlude

fatuous

cavil

insipid

phlegmatic

malinger

Sybarite, *n*.: a person addicted to luxury and pleasures of the senses. —S.C.

who: **JESSY RANDALL**

age: **24**

date: **JANUARY 1994**

where: **THE UNIVERSITY OF NORTH CAROLINA**
      at Chapel Hill

Wallowing List

"I was in library school, sharing a dumpy, insect-infested apartment with another student. Our furnace broke and it took a couple of days for the landlord to fix it. I baked a lot of biscuits to keep the apartment warm.

"I had spent the last four years at Columbia University in New York, and I missed city life very much. Chapel Hill was not what I had expected. I thought it would be a continuation of my college experience, but instead I felt like I'd gone backward—the library coursework was incredibly dull, yet ate up hours and hours; my brain was atrophying; I didn't make many friends; and I was unhappy in my love life (to put it mildly). I felt like I'd made a terrible mistake and had no one to blame but myself. I thought about dropping out of the program every single day, but never did.

"Am I a librarian now? Yes, and I have loved every library job I've ever had. Library school felt like a big waste of time while I was there, but getting that degree was well worth it. I am now the Curator of Special Collections at Colorado College, very happy in my job, and I can look back on the two years I spent in Chapel Hill and just laugh at how awful I felt. I wish I could go back and tell the twenty-four-year-old me who wrote this list not to despair, that the bad stuff would be only temporary, just like the broken furnace."

DIY LIST IDEA:

Times I've Wallowed

heat in house = make biscuits

fun in life = ?

✓ feel sorry for self

✓ become boring

✓ complain and thereby alienate others

✓ wallow

✓ make best of it but overcredit self

move

At least there were biscuits. —*S.C.*

who: A THIRTY-SOMETHING GRAD STUDENT

date: NOVEMBER 2005

where: AT HER DESK IN NEW ZEALAND

GUTSY ACTS

"When I wrote this list I was feeling overwhelmed. I had left my job at the UN and started working on a Ph.D. in a new country. At thirty-two, I was once again a (relatively) impoverished student, all my good friends were far away, and I wasn't sure if I had made the right move. I wanted to remind myself of all the risks I had taken that *had* worked out well (the first four of the list), and so included number five as a signal of hope that this move would work out just as well.

"I looked at this list fairly often until I sent it in. My life trajectory is very different from what was expected of me (husband, kids, all that conventional stuff), so when I wonder if I am on the right path or am just flailing in an attempt to carve out a meaningful life, I look at the list, remember all the funky things I have done that have emerged out of risks taken, and feel much better. I think lists like these signify attempts to impose some sort of order on an otherwise chaotic universe. Not sure if it is totally successful, but perhaps it helps somewhat."

DIY LIST IDEA:
Gutsy Things I've Done

risks I took (and that paid off) (aka. how to cheer myself up when I feel blue)

- going to grad school with only $9.00 in my bank account.
- moving to Japan when I had never been overseas
- telling Alain that I was in love with him for all of those years
- whistle-blowing on the not-so-ethical director where I worked
- quitting my job at the UN because I wasn't sure if my enviro efforts were best spent there.

Alain and the lister aren't together, but she's glad she told him. —S.C.

who: **KRUPALI TEJURA**

age: **JUST BEFORE TURNING 30**

date: **JANUARY 2006**

where: **EMORY LAW SCHOOL LIBRARY,**
Atlanta

thirty by thirty

"I am a resident physician in radiation oncology. When I wrote this list, I was just about to turn thirty and I felt frustrated. I felt that most of my life I'd lived in libraries. I wanted to see my life on paper, to see that I have done a lot, have seen the world, met leaders, and experienced life to the best of my ability. Reading it made me feel happier, to not have the dreary feeling that I've done nothing other than study."

DIY LIST IDEA:
Thirty Things to Do in the Next
Thirty Years

30 Things Accomplished By 30

1) Traveled to Galapagos Islands
2) Met Nelson Mandela
3) Learned fluent Spanish
4) Got my MD
5) Spoke at high school/med school graduation
6) Planned a surprise party for my parents,
7) Learned how to Ski
8) Hot air ballooned over the Serengeti
9) Hiked the Inca Trail
10) Went to the Oprah Show - & Sang on TV
11) Saw a Broadway Play
12) Listend/Went to 3 U2 concerts
13) Got my heart broken !!
14) Backpacked in Europe
15) Was in a burning airplane & Survived
16) Started blogging - blog quoted in Washington Post!
17) Danced on a table in VEGAS
18) Snorkled in Bermuda
19) Hanglided across the TN mountains
20) Saw USC play in the 2006 Rose Bowl (fight ON!)
21) Went to 3 funerals - Spoke at 2 of them
22) Lost 30 pounds
23) Played softball & learned how to Slide
24) Had season tix to my fave MLB team
25) Sat courtside at a Lakers Game & met Kareem Abdul Jabbar
26) Was on TV, in a magazine & newspaper
27) Read over 1000 books, (can't cant).
28) Saw Van Goghs Sunflowers in Amsterdam !!.
29) Learned to bake & cook.... .
30) Became comfortable in my skin & happy c myself!!!

How many people can say they've been in a burning airplane and survived? —S.C.

"Radical change, the kind that gives you a shot at a second or third chance, has always been my favorite fantasy."

—WENDY WASSERSTEIN, from "The Me I'd Like to Be," in Shiksa Goddess

3 NEW YEAR'S RESOLUTIONS

We have a bizarre relationship with New Year's resolutions. In late December we're bombarded with tips for thinking big, so we can become the ideal person we want to be. On the other hand, there's a growing sense of fatalism around resolutions—that if a commitment is made at New Year's, it won't work, by definition. Forty to 50 percent of Americans make annual promises to themselves. The other 50 percent boast they have given up resolutions. They're not going to spoil a holiday dedicated to debauchery with the quest for self-improvement.

Despite all the naysayers, and even though I'm nowhere near 100 percent successful, I'm still pro–New Year's resolutions—as a list holiday, if nothing else. I can't give up the delusion that change is possible, because maybe it is! At New Year's parties, I enjoy asking people what their resolutions are, encouraging them to create some if they don't have any. New Year's doesn't have to be so much about follow-through as about the excitement of that moment. It's a rare collective exercise in introspection. The other times when we make commitments tend to be far more personal, in the wake of romantic or job disasters, or at a birthday or wedding. New Year's is the only time we make big-picture lists and talk about them together.

The New Year's lists in this chapter capture that hopeful moment. They weren't necessarily tools for complete self-transformation, but that's okay. They move us toward our goals, even if they don't deliver us to the promised land of perfection. As one husband and father, whose epic list spans seven categories, puts it, "I find myself about 40 percent successful but still persist in making progress."

Resolutions also become our meta to-do lists, more valuable than everyday lists, because they become such a snapshot of the person we wanted to be at a given age. Two lists in this chapter are more than twenty years old. Maggie Trapp, in her "1983 New Year's Resolutions," written at age twelve, aspired to let her eyelashes grow, write a short novel, and compliment two people a day. Twenty-seven years earlier, sixteen-year-old Arlene Mandrell wrote her list at 11:55 p.m. 1956. She vowed to never go out with icky boys and to start every day by grinning in the mirror. Both girls wanted to be popular and found guidance for their resolutions in teen magazines. I guess some things never change!

who: **ARLENE MANDRELL**

age: **ALMOST 16**

date: **DECEMBER 31, 1956 (at 11:55 p.m.)**

A BROOKLYN TEENAGE GIRL'S RESOLUTIONS, 1956

"I wrote this list as a senior at Franklin K. Lane High School in Brooklyn. I was a cute, innocent, yet self-aware young woman, a little boy-crazy. Why did I think I should 'stop teasing boys (especially those over 18)'? Boys might not be able to control themselves, particularly if we were at a beach party. They were always bigger and stronger, and I was aware of the danger. If you got a boy 'too excited' he'd get carried away and force you to have sex. Girls like me wanted to be popular, but it was dangerous to even consider having sex in the days before the Pill. Girls who had sex ended up pregnant and had to leave school."

DIY LIST IDEA:
New Year's Resolutions I've
Actually Kept

December 31 st
11:55 P. M.

<u>New Year's Resolutions</u>

1) I will sew buttons on
as soon as they fall off

2) I will wear lipstick
whenever I leave the house

3) I will not tease boys
(especially ones over 18)

4) I will not get fat +
flabby.

5) I will start every day
off by grinning in the
mirror

6) I will not light a
cigarette if I don't really

Makes me wonder about lists from 1856. —S.C.

(Resolutions 7 through 12 on p. 235)

who: **MAGGIE TRAPP**

age: **12**

date: **1983**

where: **NEWPORT BEACH, CALIFORNIA**

Junior High
Self - Improvement

"I was in junior high in a town full of people totally unlike me but whom I wanted, at the time, desperately to be like—hence the volleyball and tennis directives, which were so clearly not about me. I was a serious devotee of *Seventeen* and *Teen* magazines, trying to 'better' myself, as evidenced by the items about complimenting at least two people per day and losing weight. The 'write a short novel' prompt sitting there unblinkingly at the end seems so outlandish and sweet at the same time, as if it were just one more thing to cross off my list at twelve.

"What strikes me now is how self-aware I was, enumerating all these things I wanted to accomplish, large and small, adding little check-off boxes in different ink, later, and then saving the list for more than twenty years. There is a real sense of nostalgia in that, which is one thing above all that I still carry with me—the urge to constantly think about what I'm doing as if I'm already looking back on it from the future. And that is of course part of the allure of to-do lists—you need them at the moment to get things in order, but you also already have in mind some future self who will look back and remember, reevaluate, this self now."

DIY LIST IDEA:
My Goals at Twelve (Be sure to write
List on Age-Appropriate Stationery)

1983
New Year's
Resolutions

☐ 1. Lose 10-15 lbs!!
☐ 2. Make at _least_
5 new friends.
③ ☐ Study hard and get all
A's.
④ ☐ Compliment _at least_
2 people everyday.
⑤ ☐ Let my eyelashes grow.
⑥ ☐ Practice hard & get
really good at volley-
ball & tennis.
⑦ ☐ Write a short novel.

"Eyelashes"? —S.C.

who: **AN ASPIRING BUDDHIST**

age: **33**

date: **JANUARY 3, 2006**

RESOLVED:
be in the present moment

"Daily meditation is my perpetual resolution. I know from experience that meditating, even just fifteen minutes a day, would make me less anxious and more compassionate, but somehow it is phenomenally difficult to do. I did meditate this past year, but not daily, probably a few times a month. I'll put it on the list again this year, but I'm fearful of another wipeout."

DIY LIST IDEA:
My Perpetual New Year's Resolutions

NYR 2006

- Daily meditation or relaxation
- cook more.
- relax, be in the present
    moment
- no sugar
- be conf. w/ age +
(ompassionate to others

Strangely ambitious for someone who's trying to relax. —S.C.

who: **SARA CAMBRIDGE**

age: **17**

date: **JANUARY 10, 1983**

where: **EVERGREEN, COLORADO**

STARTING *the* NEW YEAR *right!*

"I'm guessing this list was in response to a New Year's resolution to love myself more. I wrote it in my senior year of high school. How does it feel to read it twenty-odd years later? Initially I was amused and, of course, embarrassed by the more bizarre entries, such as 'humble for such an interesting person' and 'a personal friend of Jack Daniels, arh arh' (which is particularly odd as I've never been much of a drinker). Then it struck me that I still have many of the same qualities, but I would never phrase them that way now (i.e., 'the kind of person that makes others feel good about themselves'). Maybe what I mean is that there was a naïveté and innocence that I find touching."

DIY LIST IDEA:
My "Goodie" List

SARA'S GOODIE LIST   1/10/83

SARA IS

- PATIENT
- KIND-
- GOOD-HEARTED
- CREATIVE
- WITTY
- SELF-SUFFICIENT
- HUMAN (WHEW! I WASN'T SURE!)
- SMART
- STRONG WILLED
- HEARD WORKING
- DEDICATED
- TALENTED
- A GREAT SEWER & COOK
- THE KIND OF PERSON THAT
  MAKES OTHERS FEEL GOOD
  ABOUT THEMSELVES
- ~~SEARCH~~
- SEARCHING AND ON THE
  LOOKOUT FOR A BETTER WAY
- OPTOMISTIC
- ENTERTAINING (RESULTS ORIENTED)
- A GOOD DANCER
- OUTGOING
- CRAZY & DARING
- A WONDERFUL DRESSER
  WITH A GREAT SENSE
  OF STYLE
- HUMBLE FOR SUCH
  AN INTERESTING PERSON

- FUN!
- AMBITIOUS & SELF-IMPROVING
- A SEXY WALKER
- NOT UPTIGT
- NOT GOING TO GIVE UP
- EXPLORING HER OPTIONS
- GOING TO SELL TONS
  OF BOOKS IF IT KILLS HER
- A GREAT WRITER
- LIBERAL & INVOLVED
- OBJECTIVE
- A FAN OF MR. ROCK
  HIMSELF...EJ & BS
- A PERSONAL ~~FAN~~ FRIEND OT
  JACK DANIELS (ah ah!)
- NOT AFRAID TO ASK
  A MAN OUT (ASSERTIVE)
- NOT SATISFIED WITH
  THE STATUS QUO
- A GOOD LISTENER &
  GREAT TALKER
- APPRECIATIVE OF
  OTHER'S GOOD QUALITIES
- TRUSTWORTHY
- NOT GOING TO BE
  INTIMIDATE BY OTHERS
  BECAUSE SHE KNOWS THE
  ONLY DIFFERENCE IS THE
  EGO SIZE

Sadly, Sara says she is no longer a "sexy walker." —S.C.

who: **ERI AKBAR**

age: **25**

date: **JANUARY 6, 2005**

where: **SINGAPORE**

moving to DUBAI

"At an age when I should be living it up, I feel lifeless. My life is too structured, with not enough spontaneity and adventure. Did the list help? Yes. To me, writing a list is like inking a contract with myself. Now it's August. I broke up with G., stopped straightening my hair and let the natural curls out in full glory. I researched moving to Dubai, sent in writing for a children's book competition, took up salsa, spent more time with my family (mum is v. pleased), and so on. Some of it may be a work-in-progress but at least it has gotten off the ground."

DIY LIST IDEA:
Places I'd Like to Live for a Year

01/06/05

- ✓ Stop moping around - it's not end of the world
- challenge self and more to
- ✓ Dubai to work (do research, learn to cook, do laundry and tidy up room)
- ✓ Break up wt G - don't feel guilty and settle cos afraid will be left on shelf
- ✓ Preserve own beauty - stop straightening hair and trying to be skinny like everyone else
- ✓ Take mum out at least once a month and spoil her
- ✓ Tell friends to clean up their own mess.
- ✓ Be more tolerant of stupid people

Who knew that the quarter-life crisis was this widespread? —S.C.

who: **A HUSBAND AND FATHER**

age: **38**

date: **JANUARY 2006**

where: **WHEATON, ILLINOIS**

A FATHER'S Magic Goals

"I love resolutions, especially because so many people doubt them and make fun of that time of year when people are stirred to dream bigger. I find myself about 40 percent successful but still persist in making progress. My wife laughs at my infatuation with goals and lists. We have a long-standing joke that her disdain for my motivational stuff will someday give me extra credibility when I make it all happen.

"I've coined the phrase 'Magic Goals' because it seems like the mere act of writing down ten to twenty specific goals has the most amazing results when I look back after a given year. The magic is the wonder in discovering that cultivating strong, focused desire and committing the vision to paper makes things happen. Even folding up and hiding the paper for a year will lead to amazing discoveries. Imagine what happens when I regularly revisit and recompose the list."

DIY LIST IDEA:

Magic Goals

2006

Family
- 30 minutes/night hanging out/fun
- Date Jenn weekly
- Individual buddy time with each child weekly
- 15 minutes uninterrupted time/day with Jenn

Friends
- Specific accountability w/life group & R.F.
- Call each person weekly

Church
- Always serve: graphics, boys brigade, mentoring, helps. S.T.A.M.P. trip

Work / Finances
- 2 interviews/meetings per week
- Call database every 3 months (Jelly Bean)
- No debt
- Save 10k/yr
- Side job

Health
- 1 serving alcohol/day
- 1 free day / BFL eating
- BFL exercise

Hobbies
- Finish: Design to Delivery
- Illustrator CS2
- Photoshop 7 WOW

- 100% salary
- Save 10k/yr.
- Ø debt
- Stamp trip
- Accblty friend w/all life group & R.F.
- Self-talk list
- Finish graphics training
- 90k income
- Discover mission/purpose
- Rightness w/ $/home/location/purpose

Mentors — M-Dale, Thrsher, T. Aug., SGR
Topics: How to discover mission/purpose
Reversing fatalism, fear, discouragement (opposites of spir. gifts!) I'm an encourager but discouraged
Biggest weakness is "stuff" that ensues from work uncertainty.
Talk over "spooked" from 6 yrs of calamities
Regaining sense of simple trust, provision, answers to prayer, help, guidance, shalom, blessing.

2X month (C. Owen)

All these goals, and he still dates his wife weekly, at the local Vietnamese noodle shop. —S.C.

who: **ILENE FERNANDEZ IVINS**

age: **24**

date: **JANUARY 3, 2004**

where: **HER LOS ANGELES APARTMENT,**
   on the balcony

JUST SAY YES 2004

"'Say yes' was catchy because it refuted the slogan 'Just say no' that had been ingrained in me from the anti-drug campaign of my youth. 'Say yes' was saying yes to adventure, rule-breaking, and potentially mind-altering experiences. I wanted 'yes' to guide every decision, from little to big. (Should I try a new strategy for teaching in my classroom?)

"So, yeah, in 2004 I said yes all the time. I dated like crazy, traveled in Mexico City with my mother, and tried out great lesson plans (poetry and writers workshop) that made my spring tolerable. The motto gave me all this energy, and it was short, so it would spring into my head often. I'd be making a small decision like 'Should I try eating this weird rare venison?' and then I'd hear the little voice saying, 'Say yes,' and so I'd do it. I did gain a lot of weight in 2004 though. Not-so-great side effect."

DIY LIST IDEA:
Things to Say Yes To

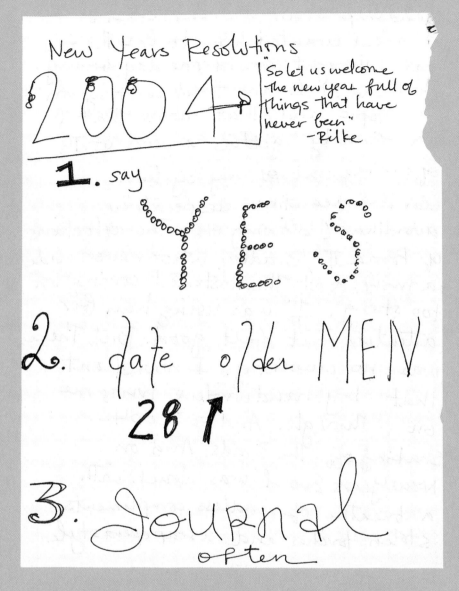

New Years Resolutions
2004

"So let us welcome
the new year full of
things that have
never been"
—Rilke

1. say

YES

2. date older MEN
28 ↑

3. Journal
often

Three *is* the magic number. —S.C.

1. Careers I would PURSUE if I didn't CARE what my friends or family THOUGHT 2. Past Jobs 3. favorite work snacks 4. Best way to Waste TIME at WORK 5. Advantages of FREELANCE Life 6. DISAdvantages of FREELANCE LIFE 7. What I would do If i Were Diagnose with cancer 8. Jobs that no Longer exist that MIGHT have been fun 9. Start-Up Business Ideas 10. What I wanted to b when I was a kid 11. Past wor place CRUSHES 12. What I want my WORKPlace Life to LOOK in FIVE years 13. What I Love About my Job 14. what Bugs me about MY Job 15. favorite

4 DREAM JOBS and bored at work

The best way to get a snapshot of someone's work life might be to peek at his or her to-do list. Is it crazed? Organized? Are there long blocks of leisure time for talks at the water cooler? These work lists give us a peek at individual job experiences: what it's like to be a therapist-in-training freaked out by the prospect of working with clients; a burned-out special-ed teacher; a man who starts churches in Montana. One of the lists, by Stephen Dubner, coauthor of *Freakonomics,* provides a look at the daily life of a high-profile journalist. I must admit, his list inspired a new feeling in me—list envy. Why can't I have "To India w/ Bill Clinton" on my list instead of "laundry," "sort lists," "count lists," etc.?

The most common work lists are inventories of chores. But the work lists I chose to include were more unexpected than productivity plans. They came from people who didn't have jobs or were unhappy with jobs they had. They were trying to figure out which path to take, how to return to a job after traveling, how to keep work from consuming them. Work holds so much promise as a way of contributing to the world and for self-expression. And yet, finding a job that's meaningful, pays well, allows you to have a life, and is not boring is not easy. It leads to a lot of list-making.

The sad reality is that most Americans don't like their jobs—87 percent are unhappy with them, according to a study cited in *Forbes.* So we look for solace in the workplace we have, whether through the company of co-workers, free soda, petty theft of office supplies, or writing personal lists on the job. That coworker who is so diligently taking notes at meetings is usually doodling or writing a personal list. The extreme sterility of a corporate job can stimulate great creativity. "Bored at Work" (page 70) is a gem, a testament to one woman's ability to document every passing thought while "working."

If you're not satisfied with writing snarky lists at a job you hate, you might try writing lists to find the right career. David Koeppel, whose "Job List" is on page 73, went on a list spree when he dropped out of grad school. Exercises from *What Color Is Your Parachute?* led him to the conclusion that he could be a "model" or a "mill supervisor." In the end, he said the list helped "in a perverse way"—after exhausting the rational systems available through list making, he went with his instinct. He's now a successful freelance journalist.

who: **A THERAPIST-IN-TRAINING**

age: **31**

date: **OCTOBER 4, 2004**

A Therapist's Fears

"This list was made at the beginning of my third year of grad school. I was studying to be a psychotherapist, working with clients of my own, and facing big struggles around entering a profession that I loved, was good at, and felt totally overwhelmed by at the same time. I like the idea of people reading this list because I think most of us need to believe that therapists always have their shit together. But shrinks are human, too.

"What did I mean when I wrote, 'I HATE having to think about clients in relation to my hair or clothes'? Every therapist I've talked to has horror stories about running into clients on the street or at the supermarket. You know, Sunday mornings when you can't be bothered to put yourself together because you're only going outside to grab a paper and a bagel. I guarantee, as soon as you become a therapist, one of your clients will be in that bagel line. And now she's seen you blushing in your tattered sweatpants and no makeup. I'm laughing now, because I realize it's not that big a deal. But it felt like a big deal at the time."

DIY LIST IDEA:
Fears About My Job

October 4, 2004
Some Truths.

I am afraid of the future
I hide a lot
I feel hopeless.
I get scared and feel closed in
when I think about making a
commitment to clients.
I look forward to terminating.
I feel like a failure for wanting
to terminate
I am so afraid that no one will
hire me.
I don't really want to be hired.
I am confused about what is
therapeutic.
I HATE having to think about
clients in relation to my
hair or clothes.
I am tired of thinking
about myself so much.

What your therapist is *really* writing while you talk . . . —S.C.

who: **A WOMAN who had just graduated
with a Masters of Public Administration
in Environmental Science**

age: **25**

date: **APRIL 13, 2006**

where: **CONNECTICUT**

Bored at Work

"I had a hard time finding a job after grad school and settled on working at a small geophysics firm. I thought it would be a challenging, engaging, productive job. I have been disappointed with my coworkers, my boss, and my position (essentially, secretary). Instead of doing fieldwork, which my boss reserves for his son and son-in-law (he is both nepotistic and sexist), I stay in the office, answer phones, and complete mind-numbingly boring tasks such as data entry.

"I wrote the list at work and hid it from my coworkers. I do all sorts of things at work that I shouldn't do (mostly surf the Internet and learn about random things). I have gotten pretty good at quickly minimizing non-work-related windows and writing to-do lists instead of taking notes at meetings. I wrote the list throughout the day, in between doing some (minimal) work. I had a few questions saved up, but most were spontaneous ponderances. I could easily write a list like that any day of the week."

DIY LIST IDEA:
My Questions of the Universe

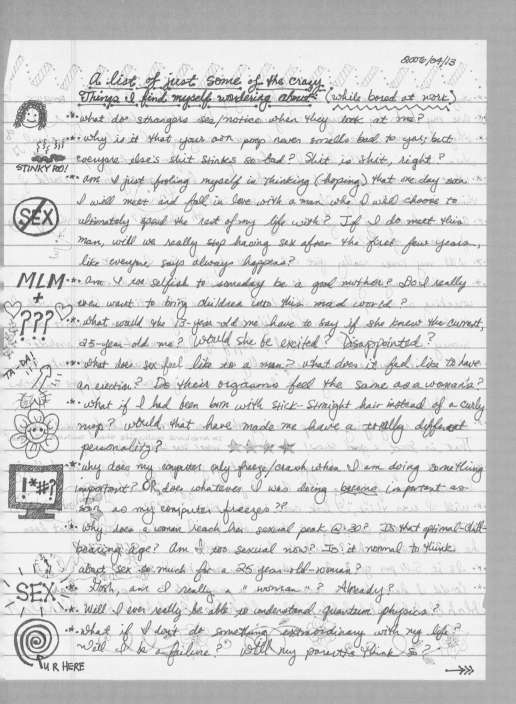

A list of just some of the crazy Things I find myself wondering about (while bored at work)

* what do strangers see/notice when they look at me?

* why is it that your own poop never smells bad to you; but everyone else's shit stinks so bad? Shit is shit, right?

STINKY POO!

* am I just fooling myself in thinking (hoping) that one day soon I will meet and fall in love with a man who I will choose to ultimately spend the rest of my life with? If I do meet this man, will we really stop having sex after the first few years, like everyone says always happens?

MLM +
♡ ??? ♡

* am I too selfish to someday be a good mother? Do I really even want to bring children into this mad world?

* what would the 13-year-old me have to say if she knew the current, 25-year-old me? would she be excited? Disappointed?

TA-DA!

* what does sex feel like to a man? what does it feel like to have an erection? Do their orgasms feel the same as a woman's?

* what if I had been born with stick-straight hair instead of a curly mop? would that have made me have a totally different personality?

* why does my computer only freeze/crash when I am doing something important? OR does whatever I was doing become important as soon as my computer freezes??

* why does a woman reach her sexual peak @ 30? Is that optimal-child-bearing age? Am I too sexual now? Is it normal to think about sex so much for a 25 year-old-woman?

SEX

* Gosh, am I really a "woman"? Already?

* will I ever really be able to understand quantum physics?

* what if I don't do something extraordinary with my life? Will I be a failure? Will my parents think so?

U R HERE

——→>>

Does *your* poop smell bad to you? —S.C.

(More crazy questions on p. 236)

who: **DAVID KOEPPEL**

age: **AFTER DROPPING OUT of grad school at 29**

date: **MARCH/APRIL 1991**

where: **LOS ANGELES**

the list helped in a perverse way

"My life was in turmoil. I dropped out of graduate school for clinical psychology and was deeply involved in the self-reflection exercises offered by the job search bible *What Color Is Your Parachute?*, which in the past I had regarded with disdain but turned out to be really helpful.

"The ranking system was a personality/career compatibility test that ranked you in six dimensions. There was a companion booklet with hundreds of jobs that were supposed to correspond. I circled jobs that I thought I might actually enjoy. Did I ever really believe that I would be a mill supervisor, shoe salesman, or model? Only in my worst nightmares. I don't know what a mill supervisor is.

"I became a freelance journalist. I started taking continuing-ed classes in writing and reporting at UCLA. I've been primarily writing for *The New York Times*, but have also written for *New York* magazine, *Entertainment Weekly,* and the *New York Post*. It's a great fit, and the list helped me in a perverse way. It made me realize I didn't need an antiquated career inventory to realize what I wanted to do with my life. I had to go with my instinct."

DIY LIST IDEA:
Jobs I Would Do if No One Paid Me /
Jobs I Wouldn't Do for a Million Dollars

$ AEC   EAC ESC ECS
AC$ ECA
ACS   AES ADE A SC
AJC   Enterprising (32) Artistic (29) Social) (29)
         SEC   EAS - ESA   C - C2D

Top Job cluster	✓* 1.	Columnist/Commentator - 6
	2.	Broker-Market Operator Grain - 5
	* 3.	Director - Council on Aging 5
	* 4.	Fashion Coordinator 5
	* 5.	Manager Housing Project 5
	6.	Field Supervisor - Seed Production - 5
	* 7.	Music Supervisor - 45
	8.	Mill Supervisor
	9.	Shoe Salesman
	10.	Supervisor - 4
	11.	Model

Social Welfare

Reporter   * 12. Administrator   6
Director   * 13. Director of Placement 6 · maybe
Writer News   14. Judge
Ad   15. Lawyer
Pub   16. Alumni Secretary
Cn.Bz   17. Artist's Manager
Ind &yth.   18. Business Rep - Labor Union
Law   *   19. Foreign Service Officer - maybe
             *   20. Director of Admissions maybe
                  21. Camp Director
✓   *   22. News Director
             *   23. Equal Opp Rep.
             *   24. Exec V.P. Chamber of Commerce
             *   25. Literary Agent
             *   26. Manager Ad Agency
             *   27. Convention Manager

What's a "Broker-Market Operator Grain"? —S.C.

who: **A BURNED-OUT NEW TEACHER**

age: **26**

date: **SPRING 2006**

SPECIAL-ED teacher on the VERGE

"I wrote this list while bored in a class for my master's in teaching. It was a major reality check for me. I've since quit teaching and am in full post-teaching recovery, focusing on me, myself, and I. While normally I might feel ashamed about focusing on myself, throughout my (short) career as a special-ed teacher, I constantly pressured myself to give to others, and it affected my happiness, not to mention my relationships. I suffered from insomnia, depression, and anxiety—all linked to my job.

"In thinking about my next job, my mantra is: No career can prevent me from doing the things on my personal list. Maybe in a few years, babies or cooking classes or home ownership will be on the list. If they are, I want a career that allows me the freedom to do those things. I feel lucky that I learned this lesson young."

> *DIY LIST IDEA:*
> *Things I'll Do When I Quit My Job*

When I'm Not A Teacher Anymore...

I WILL: (21 days left!!!)

workout in the mornings

make a proper breakfast

read books

help "at·risk" kids & families in
other cool ways so that
I can still sleep at night

not lose myself to my work so
that I can sleep at night

go out for cocktails past 9:00!

Because we should all be able to go out past nine *and* sleep at night. —S.C.

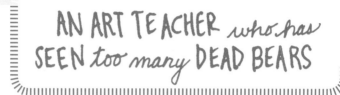

AN ART TEACHER who has
SEEN too many DEAD BEARS

"As a teaching assistant at a small state college in New York, I was surprised by how often angels, eyeballs, ponies, mermaids, Nintendo game accessories, and other imagery of this nature appeared in the artwork of undergraduate-level students. Amused and bewildered, my friends from a weekly knitting circle and I compiled a list of recurring imagery to be avoided by future students. Did I post the list in class? No, I referred to it verbally. Did the students ever fight back? Some did argue and won me over—I'm okay with unicorns, etc., when they're used in a way that is interesting."

> *DIY LIST IDEA:*
> *If I Could Wipe Five Things Off the*
> *Face of the Earth, They Would Be:*

NO IMAGE LIST

FANTASY CREATURES
Cemetaries
BOYFRIENDS / GIRLFRIENDS
Hearts
KISSING scenes

star
sun
moon
praying hands
eyes
butterflies / dragonflies
wands / swords
ponies
mermaids / fairies
puzzle pieces
MC ESCHER Reference
angels
Nintendo · game accessories
Cell phones
Ipod / Namebrands

free woman

sunset
wooden mannequins

Clock
↳ Dali-esque

D & D
Animé
Disney
Computer
Famous Musicians
Dead bears
Musical notes
Palettes / brushes
Lizards / Frogs
Dolphins
surf / skate /
snowboard
Stuffed animals

smiley faces · Religious Iconography / beach scene

Imagine all these things on one glorious canvas—
first person to send me this painting gets a prize! —S.C.

who: **BRYCE PROVO**

age: **26**

date: **MAY 2006**

where: **KALISPELL, MONTANA**

Contacting GOD

"I am helping to start a new church, a young adults' (18 to 30) church. It has been a struggle, but it's rewarding to know I am doing what I was placed on earth to do. Planting churches can be very discouraging. People come to the church with an attitude of 'What can I get?' instead of 'What do I have to give to others?' Money is a constant nag in the back of your mind because of the shoestring budgets that new churches have. Volunteers can be unreliable, or worse, unpredictable. People seem to come out of the woodwork to criticize and offer unhelpful advice. Just when you think that it's all going to fall apart, a check comes to pay a bill, or somebody dedicated and capable steps up to fill a needed position. It all seems to work out, just at the last minute. Prayer is mentioned twice to remind myself that it is the most important thing to do. After all, the main point of church is to help people to contact God."

DIY LIST IDEA:
Religions I Would Like to Start

To start a New Church:

1. Pray
2. Find Worship leader
3. Find building
4. Advertise
5. Talk to people - locals
   - Find needs in community
   - Find interests in community
6. gather core-group for planning
7. Place all ministries
   - children, outreach, greeters, youth, etc.
8. grand-opening service
9. Pray

Does prayer help get things done? —S.C.

who: **STEPHEN DUBNER, coauthor of the best-selling book** *Freakonomics*

date: **SEPTEMBER 4, 2006**

where: **NEW YORK CITY**

behind the scene of
FREAKONOMICS

"The first item, 'Finish NYT/Handwash': Steve Levitt and I write a 'Freakonomics' column for the *New York Times Magazine*—this one was about the difficulty in getting doctors to properly wash their hands between patients.... The third item, '9/18 Google visit—wait to hear from ABC': Finalizing a visit to Google headquarters in California for some research. Was pending the go-ahead from ABC's *20/20,* since I'd proposed doing an hour-long show on Google.... The fifth item, 'ECFS application': Applying my daughter to kindergarten at Ethical Culture Fieldston School. The essay would take nearly as long as writing the *N.Y. Times* column.... The twelfth item, 'NYT revise (Bender quote)': In revise of *NYT* column, had to add some context to one doctor's quote. 'ECFS finalize': Still working on that damn kindergarten application.... 'Nov 29, 30, Dec. 1. India w/ Bill Clinton? (Delhi, Bombay, Bangalore)': Possible lecture tour of India, warming up for Bill Clinton. (We have the same lecture agent; lucky me.)"

DIY LIST IDEA:
Articles I'd Write for
The New York Times

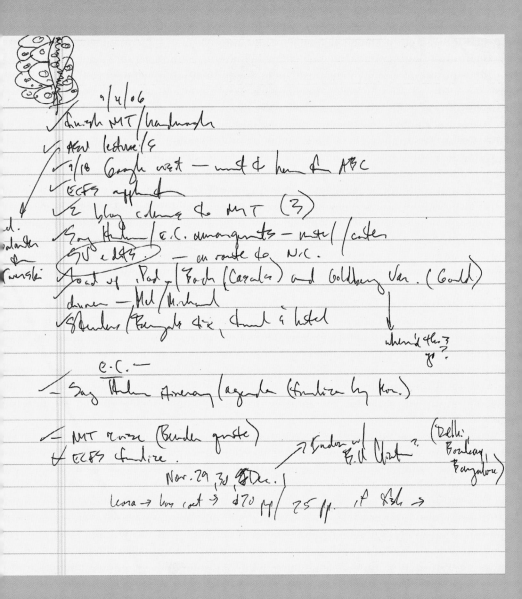

HANDWRITING TRANSLATION:

Finish NYT/Handwash
ASU lecture/s incl. Salanter from Twerski
9/18 Google visit—wait to hear from ABC
ECFS application
2 blog columns to NYT (3)
Sag Harbor / E.C. arrangements—motel/cater
SV edits—en route to N.C.
Load up iPod w/ Bach (Casals) and Goldberg
   Var. (Gould) Where'd this go?

Dinner—Mel/Michael
Steelers/Bengals tix, travel and hotel
E.C.—Sag Harbor itinerary/agenda
   (finalize by Mon.)
NYT revise (Bender quote)
ECFS finalize
Nov 29, 30, Dec. 1. India w/ Bill Clinton?
   (Delhi, Bombay, Bangalore)
Leora has cost $20 pp/25 pp if fish

"India w/ Bill Clinton"? I have list envy. —S.C.

who: **NICK HORNBY**, author of *High Fidelity,*
a novel about an obsessive list-maker

date: **SUMMER 2003**

where: **LONDON**

desert island DISCs

"I'm actually not a great list-maker even though some of my characters are, but I did find this in a notebook. I was invited on to a famous British radio program called *Desert Island Dises,* and was trying to work out which eight records I'd like to take with me to a desert island. I was almost paralyzed by the task until I hit on the idea of taking an iPod as my luxury item, thus rendering the list pretty much redundant. Anyway, this was my first stab at it, because only three or four made the final cut."

DIY LIST IDEA:
Songs That Make My Heart Stop

D.I.D.

1) Lo - Night Ride Home
2) Dan - Fatou Yo Toure Kunda (World Playground)
3) Kitty's Back
4) You Wear It Well
5) The Love You Save
6) McG / Telephone Rd
7) Cali
8) ~~That be lost~~
9) Marah

Those who can't make lists write bestselling books about characters who can. —S.C.

who: **KELDA LARSEN**

age: **27**

date: **MAY 2004**

where: **KUTA BEACH, BALI**

PROS and CONS of a new JOB

"I was almost finished traveling in Asia, surfing every day and thinking about where my life was going next. I was torn between wanting to make a lot of cash doing something adventurous, and wanting to set up a stable home and community. An at-sea fisheries observer goes onboard commercial fishing boats and monitors their catches, making sure they're complying with regulations. The pay is supposed to be pretty good. But I was ready to send roots down. Fisheries observer work is supposed to be really lonely. This list may have solidified my thoughts. Before I made a decision, I was offered a job guiding sea kayak trips in Baja. The list made me realize that being connected to people was more important to me than making money."

DIY LIST IDEA:
Weird Jobs I've Had

AT-SEA FISHERIES OBSERVER

⊕	⊖
no $ worries b/c starts Jan. 17th	can't work out
no rent + food expense	can't find a boyfriend probably
The winter ocean + the coast	so maybe no sex again
~~———————~~	losing touch w/ Courtenay + then no one to go on trip w/
don't have to look for a shit job	
take the summer off to paddle, hike, party, surf, festival	more lonely
come out w/ 12 grand + can buy anything i want - clothes CD's computer tattoos, gear	might be a lot of appl. effort for nothing
flexible + can be picked up again	let down Paul + Miche but they'd understand
north B.C. coastal port stops	can't party in Courtenay
time to write?	no writing support
to set up in Van	possibly no time to write but hey probably
sure	visit Dad + Liza when?
nice challenge to get in	
ppl. gives me something to do in Bali	

Thirteen pros vs. eleven cons, but she still didn't take the job. —S.C.

"In Literature, as in Love, WE are ASTONISHED by what is chosen by OTHERS."

—André Maurois

5 Ideal Mates

Love and lists may seem like an unlikely combination. Why do two people connect? It's one of the great mysteries of life and shouldn't be too rationally understood. A person's soul could never be bullet-pointed in a list. And yet many of the lists sent to me concern romantic love. Many spell out a vision for an ideal mate. (Most of them came from women, surprise, surprise.)

Why have ideal-partner lists become so common? Anyone who dates online knows that we are living in an era of soul-mate shopping. Often the lists people post are extremely long and disturbingly specific. Although these ideal mate lists can also be hilariously long (in "Criteria" we find a request for a man who "darns his own socks"), these lists strike me as a different breed than online ads—not so much a demands letter as a private guide for navigating the partner search. The people who wrote them may have intense mathematical formulas for the percentage a potential mate needs to fulfill (usually 70 percent) but they generally store these lists in their diaries, as guides, and don't seem to demand absolute compliance.

While there's always the danger of becoming too attached to our ideal-mate lists, they can also help us to get in touch with what we want, and help those of us who have a tendency to settle to hold out for what we really want. Mostly, our urge to list a dream partner comes from our need to believe that love is possible. That after a break-up it is possible to find someone we'll click with better, that in a long dry spell, such a person could be out there. So much of success in love, or in anything, is the belief that success is possible—putting a list down on paper, or hearing a friend describe your ideal mate (an "envision session," my friend Halo calls it) is fantasy, but productive fantasy. It feeds our optimism. Pessimism is already available in droves when we're looking for love.

It's popular among New Age types to say that writing down your intentions can help to manifest your reality. Is that true in love? Maybe. I wouldn't count on a Wo/Man of Your Dreams Checklist delivering Ms./Mr. Right. But at the least, writing down what you want in a partnership forces you to think more clearly about what you want. In matters of love and lust, thinking clearly is no small accomplishment.

who: **ELIZABETH SWEENEY**

age: **21**

date: **SPRING 2002**

where: **MONTREAL**

ISO A SOCK-DARNER

"Why is it important that my future boyfriend darn his own socks? It says a lot about a person. Instead of throwing something out just because it's old and tattered, you will care for it. It says that you're going to take care of it yourself, instead of getting someone else to do it for you. It's a profound action. Obviously, the list is not an absolute. I'm not going to avoid someone if they don't hum or plan on saving the world. But it helps me remember what's important to me. I don't think I'm looking for anything unattainable here."

DIY LIST IDEA:
My Ideal Mate

~~MAN~~ CRITERIA

- darns his own Socks
- plays me Songs
- lights camp fires
- laughs
- Smiles
- Hums
- Keeps me warm
- ~~Hates~~ his own plans

- likes to get his hands dirty.
- ~~likes~~ walks

- Thinks.
- Thinks well
- loves
- loves well
- Spontaneous.

- tea-drinking.
- apple eater
- reasonable
- Happy
- Modest
- Bridge builder.
- Hard Worker
- Honest and True
- buys me good used Books on a whim.
- 10. Save the world
- considerate
- daring and decisive
- assertive and cooperative.
- Naps occasionally.

Who comes close? Pete Seeger (she thinks). I guess he darns his own socks. —S.C.

who: **JACOB ALLRED**

age: **18**

date: **AUGUST 2003**

where: **FLORENCE, SOUTH CAROLINA**

a YOUNG MORMON's
Ideal Woman

"I was just sitting, thinking, one day and started to think of what attributes my ideal wife would have. I'm not talking about stuff like beautiful eyes, great kisser, or anything like that, but more along the lines of what that person chooses to do. And I'm not saying that even I fulfill my ideal attributes. I know I have some stuff I need to work on, so don't go contacting me saying I'm a hypocrite, because I'm not. This is simply a list of what I would like my wife to be like, not necessarily what anyone is capable of."

DIY LIST IDEA:
What I Thought I Wanted in a Mate
at Eighteen

My Ideal Mate

Items are in no particular order.

Doesn't smoke, drink alcohol, drink coffee, use illegal drugs, or abuse legal drugs.

Is a member of The Church of Jesus Christ of Latter-day Saints and is worthy to enter the temple.

Understands what finance charges are and avoids them like the plague.

Doesn't want dogs, birds, rabbits, or snakes as pets.

Puts trash in the proper waste receptacle.

Doesn't drink excessive amounts of soda.

Brushes twice daily. And flosses.

Doesn't use foul language, including foreign curse words or taking the Lord's name in vain.

Doesn't steal.

Accepts responsibility for their actions.

Reads the scriptures every day.

Wants to have children.

Looks forward to having Family Home Evening.

Can cook at least a few good meals.

Doesn't watch inappropriate movies, even if they do have a PG-13 rating.

Is comfortable with who they are, even if they aren't wearing makeup or looking their best.

Has a college degree (or is working towards one), and supports me in my continuing education.

Rinses her dirty dishes and puts them in the dishwasher.

Separates darks from whites before doing laundry.

Uses nice smelling shampoo.

Doesn't burn incense.

Is not a member of the Democratic Party.

Regularly goes to church.

Pays tithing.

Avoids music that promotes inappropriate activities or contains foul language.

Likes chick-flicks and drags me to them even if I pretend I don't want to see them.

Will let me give my first son the middle name of "Jacob."

Chews with her mouth shut.

Doesn't care if I wear the same tie every Sunday.

Enjoys picnics.

Uses her turn signal when appropriate and turns her headlights on when it is dim outside.

Will make me tomato soup and a grilled cheese sandwich when I am sick.

Can keep a secret.

Proper use of turn signals is definitely key to a healthy relationship. —*S.C.*

who: **KATIE PLUMB**

age: **11, after her parents separated**

date: **MARCH 13, 1992**

where: **HILLIARD, OHIO**

an eleven-year-old girl's
PERFECT *husband*

"Even though it sounds so Psych 101, I'm pretty sure the list had to do with my dad. I was in fifth grade when I wrote it. My parents had separated for a year, and I was learning about my dad's affairs. (My parents got back together at the end of that summer.)

"Who was Anthony? He sat across from me in our five-desk formations. He was nice to me, and even though I don't think he was particularly good looking, he had dark skin and light blue eyes, which I thought were beautiful.

"I don't want to jinx things, but I'm pretty sure I've found my 'perfect husband.' He's easily the funniest guy I've dated, very creative and artistic. The funny thing is, some of the characteristics I like best about him are what I liked best about my dad, who died in January '95. He's probably one of the only guys I've dated whom my dad would have really liked."

DIY LIST IDEA:
Childhood Crushes I still Think About

Perfect husband

Katie Plumb
11 Mar 13 1992

1. Italian American (Like Anthony)
2. light brown hair
3. blue eyes
4. in good shape (good athlete)
5. good college education
6. ~~education~~ not a smoker
7. taller than me (6"3)
8. didn't meet him in a bar
9. never been in jail
10. respects me as an independent woman.
11. never been married — no kids from marrige before
12. wants kids (3)
13. friends arent sleezes
14. sensitive
15. shares alot of my interests
16. has a good job and doesnt work where I do.
17. will live in a beach house in California.
18. about 30 years old
19. likes puppies
20. kind dancing (fun)
21. doesn't drink (at all!)
22. good tempered

My fave requirement: Respects me as an independent woman. —S.C.

who: **A WOMAN** trying to figure out whether to
get back together with her ex-boyfriend

age: **34 WHEN SHE WROTE THE LIST,** 35 when
she made the purple checkmarks

date: **SEPTEMBER 22, 2004**

where: **BERKELEY, CALIFORNIA**

twenty-*seven*
OUT OF *forty*-*two*

"I was single when I wrote this list of my vision for the perfect mate. Then, years later, my ex-boyfriend, who had dumped me, said he wanted to get back together. So I went to the list and made the purple checkmarks to figure out if I should. He got twenty-seven out of forty-two—over half. But, of course, by then I had already decided to get back together with him. He dumped me again about a year ago (a year after we got back together). Now he wants me back again. I don't need a checklist anymore to know that's not such a great idea!"

DIY LIST IDEA:

Exes

9/22/04   My Vision of The Perfect Mate

Male ✓
Employed ✓
Enjoys Reading ✓
Politically Leftist ✓
Sarcastic Sense of humor ✓
Can also be silly ✓
Takes care of how he looks, but not vain. ✓
Believes in Making responsible choices ✓
Enjoys modern culture but not obsessed
Able to be emotionally supportive
~~Enjoys~~ ~~Enjoys~~ Enjoys good food ✓
Likes to be physically active
has travelled & Wants to travel further ✓
Affectionate ✓
Loves to laugh ✓
Thinks im hot ✓
Gets along w/ his mother
Doesn't want Kids ✓

Adventurous
Understands how to listen
Self reflective
Knows how to take care of himself. ✓
Enjoys learning new Things
Attractive to me ✓
Knows how it is to be an outsider ✓
Enjoys drinking + other substances, In Moderation
Omnivore ✓
Intelligent about money but not a tightwad ✓
Gets along with at least some of his exes.
Doesn't have Kids ✓
Lives in The East Bay ✓
Practices an art ✓
Has strong Values & tries to live by them ✓
Adaptable
Open-minded
Likes to give but also receive ✓
Creative ✓
Needs alone time
Knows how to listen

Enjoys reading ✓
Gets along with animals
Wants a LTR, eventually, but not desperate ✓
                                  Total: 42
27

It's always good to start with the basics: male and employed. —S.C.

who: **SHANNON O'LEARY**

age: **EARLY THIRTIES**

date: **EARLY 2006**

where: **SAN FRANCISCO**

SOUL-mate MATH

"I composed my list after talking with my friend Dean. After much dating, he met his partner, Mark, and decided, 'This could work!' when Mark met 80 percent of his conditions. Since they've been together over ten years, I thought it was worth a shot. I have been using it for six months. I think the Man of My Dreams checklist is a good reality check on the person who has your hormones all revved up. While I haven't met him yet, I have more clarity about who he is and isn't."

DIY LIST IDEA:
My Non-negotiables

Man of My Dreams, which I will meet and be with in a committed relationship with by
_____.

1. We have completely out of this world, rip each other's clothes off, chemistry together*
2. Makes over 60K a year.
3. Ambitious
4. Artistic/Creative
5. Kind
6. Pursues me ardently and aggressively
7. 6 feet tall or over
8. Moderate drug and alcohol user
9. A rock star and/or a ninja in his chosen pursuits and vocation.
10. 32 – 43
11. Crazy about me*
12. Funny/Sarcastic*
13. Just the right balance of taking things slow and having fun but interested in meeting not just any person but the RIGHT person to commit to.
14. We are both completely ourselves around each other and become best friends pretty quickly. WE TOTALLY GET EACH OTHER.*
15. Does not have or want to have children.
16. Counter culture
17. Financially responsible and values nice things (dinners, possessions, etc)
18. Takes care of himself physically and mentally
19. Handsome/Attractive
20. Supports my creative work in either a participatory or a supportive role.

*These qualities are pretty much non-negotiable
** 70% of these qualities ensures dream man status while 60 – 65% of these qualities with the inclusion of ALL non-negotiables is acceptable.

It's nice to finally know what percentage ensures dream-man status. —S.C.

who: **CLAUDIA HECHT**

age: **29**

date: **CIRCA 1998**

PERSONAL ad Draft

"Oh God, I did post a version of this; in the *newspaper;* it was actually physical. I posted a few of these unique-style ads. I had another one about being a snake-handler. I found that the unique ones don't get a high response rate. In the future I tended to bland my ads down. People just think it's too much. How would someone else see this? I like earlobes, too! I don't know, I never figured out how to write the 'right' kind of personal ad."

DIY LIST IDEA:
Things I Love That Make Me Unique

IN LOVE

I love
words, adventure,
travelling, writing,
following my passions,
sweet
men, art, outdoors,
poetry, warm eyes,
hiking, mystery,   Scratch-n-sniff
reading,
goosebumps, trees,
(kissing, sushi)
earlobes, murals,
camping, hands,
SF 29 Call me.

HIDDEN TREASURE

SMART GIRL

SMART GIRL

SMART GIRL   SMART GIRL

SMART GIRL

I love
trees, mystery, sweet men, writing
kissing, sushi, earlobes, mountains
murals, scratch-n-sniff,
camping, goose bumps, Leaves of Grass
lemons, warm eyes, yoga
hands, sweat, dancing,
quilts, hot springs, rambling, diners,
blues, raffles, hidden treasure

the little prince

dreams of swimming, caves, wombs

She certainly had no doubt about the headline. —S.C.

who: **WADE BEESLEY**

age: **26**

date: **CIRCA JUNE 1996**

where: **AT MOJO'S DAILY GRIND, a café**
he owns and operates in Austin

Ready To Meet You

"At the time I was a hopeless romantic, wanting to find this mythical one person. I now believe we all have lots of soul mates. I used the list as a guideline, but now it's in my subconscious. I don't need a list anymore. By knowing myself better, things seem to fall into place. Have I met anyone who has come close? The woman I'm with now meets every one of the requests I made. I do think writing a list of your ideal lover is generally a 'girl' thing. Women have been socially trained to find a man, get married, and have a child. So of course they are gonna think about it more and make lists. Men think about career, sports, and beer. I'm not a typical male."

DIY LIST IDEA:
Things Someone Should
Know if We're Dating

5-24-96

♀: thin, intelligent, free-thinking, individual, no phonies, no goal in life to be cool, cute feet, small breasts bonus, 2 out of 3 a must; eat meat, drink, smoke pot; creative non-christian, sexual connection, as kinky-as-me, maybe a little more, will assist ~~allow~~ me to fulfill all my

sexual fantasies, and include me in hers, tattoos & piercings are cool not necessary, no face except nose, cute feet, small butt very very open minded but no zealots, spirituality & astrology again no zealots, creative, motivated, rich parents bonus, but must be cool, alternative wedding, no niños, wants to travel, wants to escape America as soon as possible. — Ready for commitment. I want to meet you. —

"Cute feet" must have been important to Wade. —S.C.

who: **RIMA IVALIA**

age: **23**

date: **JANUARY 2006**

where: **WEST JAKARTA, INDONESIA**

Chubby is more **Preferred**

"I met The Guy one month after I wrote these love resolutions. We've been steady since Valentine's Day. He met about 90 percent of the characteristics. Is he chubby? Yes, and getting fatter! He's a bachelor in Air Transport Management and his GPA is 3.6 out of 4.0. Did the list help me find him? It kind of sorted guys I met. If someone had below 70 percent, I quit seeing him and said, 'Let's just be friends.'"

DIY LIST IDEA:
Text Messages I've Gotten and Loved

No
Date

Januari 2006

✥ Resolusi cinta 2006 & kriteria ✥

❋1 gue tidak akan mau dengan orang-orang yang pernah
     menyakiti hati atau menolak gue sengaja maupun tidak
     sengaja.

❋2 gue tidak akan mau dengan cowo yang berumur sama,
     Paling enggak dia harus kelahiran tahun 1981.

❋3 Harus selalu bawa kendaraan, min. bawa motor.

❋4 Sudah bekerja tetap, Lulusan IT, S1, MI, Design Grafis,
     Design Interior dan Arsitektur (min. S1) IPK min. 2,8
     sangat disarankan.

❋5 Berat badan minimal Ideal, Kalo bisa chubby, gak Perlu
     ganteng gg penting enak diliat (b'pakaian stylish sangat disarankan)
     suara enak didengar, sering nelp, dan SMS, Humoris dan enak
     diajak ngobrol.

❋6 gak suka Flirting ke cewe lain, Harus setia dan tidak me-
     nganut TTM !!! ☺

❋7 Tinggal di daerah Jakarta Barat (Tangerang Termasuk deh
     ...) Tinggal di wilayah Kebon Jeruk sangat disarankan...

Amien!

KENKO® 30 Lines, 6 mm

TRANSLATION: THE 2006 LOVE RESOLUTIONS AND CRITERIA

1. I never want a guy who hurts me with or without any purpose.
2. I never want a guy who's the same age as me. At least he is born in 1981.
3. He always rides a car or a motorcycle.
4. He has been working in a company. Bachelor in Information Technologies, Information Systems, Information Management, Graphic Design, and Architecture Engineering with minimum GPA 2.8 out of 4.0 is highly recommended.
5. Has an ideal weight, chubby is more preferred. Doesn't have to be charming but he has to be good-looking (has a good sense in fashion is highly recommended), has a good voice, calls and sends texts regularly, humorist and communicative.
6. He has to be faithful. I don't want a guy who likes flirting with another girl and has other "too close girlfriends."
7. He lives in West Jakarta (Kebon Jeruk region is highly recommended). Tangerang is included.

"Amien" is similar to "amen." Indonesian Muslims say it after they pray. —S.C.

who: **STEPHANIE LIPECKY**

age: **31**

date: **APRIL 2002**

where: **AUGUSTA, GEORGIA**

SEARCH fatigue

"I wrote this list after my divorce from my first husband, to whom I was married ten years. Where I live, in Augusta, Georgia, it was extremely hard to meet a decent single man, much less one who met all my criteria. The only available guys were too young and immature, older men who had been divorced several times and had kids, or total rednecks. About a year later, I did meet a wonderful man who, although he didn't meet all my criteria, ended up being the best thing that ever happened to me! He's 5' 7" and has a daughter *and* a psycho ex!"

DIY LIST IDEA:
What I've Learned to Live With
(and Even Embrace)

Things I am looking for in a man (which is probably why I'll be single for the rest of my life)

No kids
Not married (hah hah)
Not a redneck
No hunting
No confederate flags
No racial slurs
No pyscho ex
Must have been broken up w/ the ex for at least 4-6 months - not still hung up on her
~~Have own house~~
Makes good $
~~Athletic~~
Works out
Over 5'8" (The taller the better)
Likes cats
Likes to go out / dine out
Considerate
Nice body
Doesn't have a 4 × 4
As smart as me ~~(but not a bore)~~
College grad w/ good job
Likes sports
Not a womanizer
Good track record (not a cheat)
Believes in God yet not a holy roller

The lesson: Make the list, then let fate step in. —S.C.

who: **SUE VITTNER**

age: **27**

date: **OCTOBER 2000**

where: **PORTLAND, MAINE**

Red-State Blue-State
Romance

"I made this list with my women's group. We were all in relationships that weren't doing well. That guy and I broke up. That's when I went to Antarctica and met Charlie. There are scientists doing research; you go work to support them and save up to travel. It's kind of like being in college again. I was a janitor.

"At first it wasn't *This is the person I have been searching for.* Charlie is from a really small town in Texas, and I'm from Rhode Island. I do massage therapy, yoga, meditation. He's more Republican; he hunts. He grew up ranching and I grew up going to the mall. Long after we started living together I found this list and realized there are many things on it that are true about him but not in the way I imagined. You have a person in mind when you write a list like this, but I never imagined Charlie.

"He's strong, but he doesn't work out. He's strong from work. Validates my cooking? When I cook, it's vegetables and brown rice, and he would rather have meat. He does love garlic. He'll eat it raw. He knows it will help him feel better if he has a cold. No snoring—he doesn't snore, and he doesn't mind *my* snoring. Cuddler? Yes."

DIY LIST IDEA:
Attractions That Surprised Me

THE LIST

10/31/00

| What it means to love |

To care — nurture (plant)
To be responsible — to be able to respond to needs expressed/not expressed   avail. & aware
To respect — honor, validate
Knowledgable — desire to know self, me, humanity, world   seeking

Cultivate self 1st

<u>Face</u> — nice teeth, eyes, skin, hair, part time glasses
<u>Age</u> — 27-32
<u>height</u> — taller than me, not wicked tall   5'7"-6'3"

<u>hair</u> — head hair, not lot of body hair, scruff - willing to shave for spec. occasion
    no tatoo, peircing - (trendy)
<u>body</u> — bigger than me, some muscles - from work/acrivities   no gym
    nice butt!
<u>Sports</u> — mello   ultimate frisbee, outdoor sports - hiking - water - kayak or surf   not too inhbit.
    balance   yoga, meditation (not trendy - truly)   genuine

<u>TV</u> — No sports TV watching, little or no TV
    enjoys renting movies

    Simple life, low Maintanance — No frills

<u>Kids</u> — No past kids, wants kid & to adopt

<u>drinking/drugs</u> — drinks on special occasions
    pot 1-2 times year (if any)
    not pill popper (no chemicals - few when necessary)
    <u>No</u> cigarettes smoking

<u>Creative</u> — artistically / musically / some way
    appreciates art
    galories   Live - folky, blues, jazz, world music

Don't we all want someone with part-time glasses? —S.C.

("The List" continues on p. 237)

who: **MARK A.**

age: **36**

date: **NOVEMBER 2001**

where: **AT A CAFÉ**

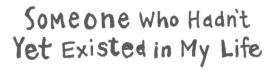

Someone Who Hadn't Yet Existed in My Life

"As part of a 12-step AA program, my sponsor had me take a look at my past sexual relations to see what had worked and what hadn't. Once the list was complete, the idea was that I should be willing to grow toward that ideal myself. The initial concept was daunting, but once I got rolling, it became really fun and creative. I kinda felt like a sculptor—creating a vision for something (er, someone) that hadn't yet existed in my life. A few months later, I started dating more frequently off Match .com and eHarmony. Thanks to my list, I could sum up pretty quickly (in fifteen minutes) whether I was interested in continuing to see someone. The list also allowed me to consider the types of relationships I *didn't* want. I met my wife two years later and she is 95 percent of the things on my list! I am so grateful I didn't settle. She rocks!"

DIY LIST IDEA:
Lessons I've Learned from
Previous Relationships

Sexual Ideal

I Physical

- LITTLE TO NO MAKEUP
- ALL NATURAL LOOKS
- LONG STRAIGHT HAIR
- SLIM TO ATHLETIC TO AVERAGE
- FRESH-FACED; A LITTLE SHORTER THAN ME; ATHLETIC NOT AFRAID TO GET DIRTY; NICE SMILE, EYES, + HANDS; HIGH LIBIDO, NOT PASSIVE; GYMNASTIC BUILD; NO FACIAL HAIR; NO HAIRY ARMS; SLIGHTLY TAN SKIN, SMOOTH, SOFT; FULL LIPS;

~~ILLEGIBLE~~

LOW MAINTENANCE; READY-TO-GO IN MINUTES; CASUAL DRESS — TSHIRT + JEANS/OVERALLS/CINDA GIRL; NOT FRILLY OR TOO GIRLY; JOGGER (GYM, YOGA EXERCISE TOGETHER); KNOWS HER BODY + ITS CYCLES;

~~ILLEGIBLE~~ SMILING EYES; LONG SLENDER FINGERS, TOES + TONGUE!;

II Mental

- SMART, INTELLIGENT, BUSINESS-SAVVY (ANALYTICAL), GOOD w/ #'S + FIGURES (EQUAL TO OR MORE EDUCATION THAN ME; POSITIVE OUTLOOK + THINKING "GLASS 1/2 FULL TYPE"; HIGHLY COMMUNICATING; HIGH DEGREE OF INTEGRITY; HONEST, TRUTHFUL, GREAT SENSE OF HUMOR (NOT AFRAID OF CHEESY LOW-BROW HUMOR); HOBBIES: MUSIC, EXERCISE, READ + WRITING PERSONAL THOUGHTS, ESPN'S; NON-FICTION BOOKS;

~~ILLEGIBLE~~

COMPASSIONATE LISTENER; ALERT + AWARE OF HER SURROUNDINGS; TO KEEP ME ON MY TOES; SHE CAN GIVE ME SHIT IN A CONSTRUCTIVE WAY; ABILITY TO RELATE TO KIDS, OTHER PEOPLE, ANIMALS + "DIFFERENCES"; HAS MALE + FEMALE FRIENDS; LAUGHS EASILY

(over →)

After twenty years of dating, Mark knew what he wanted! —S.C.

1. Communication Problems were having 2. Things that drive me crazy 3. Qualities I would like in a connection 4. Things I love about X 5. Fun first dates 6. Fun One hundredth dates 7. Boys I have loved 8. Girls I have loved 9. Crushes 10. Favorite moments in a relationship 11. Pros and Cons about X 12. Fantasies I should Retire 13. Fears about being alone 14. what it means to love 15. Qualities I Possess (why someone would want to be with me) 16. Lessons learned in Past

6 Relationships

Lists usually represent a desire for control and rationality—the exact opposite state of being in love, obsessed, or otherwise involved with another human being. So it's no wonder that so many lists are about romantic relationships, written at every phase: from the first butterfly-inducing stages (Should I ask her out?) to the end, when the wreckage of a relationship is everywhere (pros-and-cons lists with far more cons than pros). We write lists in the midst of long-term relationships that are going well, too: Here's what I'm getting that I like and here's what I want. ("You not work on weekends." "You buy me a surprise present.")

Why is it so compelling, even necessary, to jot down in item form what real love should mean, or the communication problems that *must* be discussed? We receive no formal training in how to have a relationship. Frankly, many of us are clueless. We fumble around trying to figure out how to deal with conflict, or tell someone how we really feel in the grip of extreme emotions: hope, fear, longing, lust. Listing provides a moment of rationality (or exposed irrationality), even if for just a moment on the page.

A list can be essential at the end of a relationship. If a friend is stuck in a bad relationship, always complaining but never taking action, tell him or her to make a pros-and-cons list. It's harder to stay when the reality of an overwhelmingly long cons list stares you down.

Lists can also be love poems. The what-I-love-about-you list is a way to salute all the small daily details one person loves about another. Stephanie Lipecky (who describes her search on p. 118) wrote one for her then-boyfriend, now-husband Garret as a one-year-dating-anniversary present. With all its details of what Stephanie loved about Garret—"the way you always make everything seem okay," "your teeth," "the way my heart skips a beat when a 394 number comes up on the caller ID"—her list made a few of my friends swoon. One night I was out with my friend Cameron and showed her Stephanie's list. We came up with the phrase "Garret Love" to describe the standard set by it. In the future, we imagine people will use Garret Love as shorthand in their dating profiles to describe the kind of relationship they're seeking. People will ask, "Is it Garret Love?" If not, they'll either work on the relationship or get out to find something that is.

who: **A WOMAN IN HER MID-THIRTIES**

date: **CIRCA 2004**

together: **ABOUT FOUR YEARS**

next holiday a
Wrapped present

"This list seems a little unbalanced, like I wasn't getting much that I liked, but I think that I was just focusing on what I wanted to change. It seems a little sadder than it was: Next holiday a wrapped present? Some things I said I would like I'm getting more of now. And some things I wanted and don't get don't bother me as much anymore. Did I articulate these things? Yes. Since then I have gotten a wrapped present."

DIY LIST IDEA:
What I Want More of in My Relationship

things I'm getting / like

genous
take me out to dinner
hold hands
very affectimate/snuggly

things I would like
you buy me a surprise present
~~one~~ next holiday a wrapped gift
  you initiate sex
    you tell me I look beautiful
  you turn off the cell phone on dates
  you not work on weekends
    you look into my eyes and tell me you love me
      you make plans for an evening & surprise me
        you write me a love letter
          you ~~act out~~ tie me up during sex

Four years in, she wanted surprises. —S.C.

who: **JENNY BITNER**

age: **29**

date: **CIRCA 1997**

where: **AT A TEMP JOB**

Workplace Crush

"I was working a terrible temp job at a hospital. People would call and leave messages about medical equipment. I would transcribe and help fill orders. There was a very cute girl with really short hair working in the cafeteria. I would give her little drawings and notes—a drawing of her giving me coffee, things like that. I wrote this pros-and-cons list to figure out what to do. After weighing the options, I used a pink highlighter to mark what I decided were the four most important ideas. I marked them to emphasize that I should focus on them.

"Did I ask her out? Yes. How did I feel? Nervous. I was putting all my excess creative energy into writing her notes and drawings, thinking about what she felt about me. She said yes. I think we went on a hike. I just remember feeling it wasn't going to go anywhere; she wasn't interested. I wasn't really either. It felt more like a friendship. She was nice, but I didn't feel the same erotic attraction outside the charged atmosphere of the cafeteria."

DIY LIST IDEA:
Should I Ask Him or Her Out?

Should I ask her out?

+

'd be brave
he might come
t'd be fun

don't want to be a wimp

be mad at me if I don't

So what!

ll never know till you ask

Spring love & lust are fun

—

She might say no

I'm nervous

maybe she has a girlfriend/
                    boyfriend

maybe she's straight

this is silly and overly romantic

I'm so high on caffeine I can't think
                              straight

She's too young
It would be scary

It all comes down to "So what!" in the end. —S.C.

who: **A WOMAN who makes pros-and-cons lists for all major decisions**

age: **IN HER MID-FORTIES**

date: **APRIL 2001**

where: **CINCINNATI**

Sleeping on the couch

"At the time, I was trying to accept that divorce might be the solution, no matter how much I didn't want my marriage to be a failure. I was a wreck. But I was trying to turn my emotions around from anger and humiliation, to become someone who would survive and realize it was the right choice to let him get the divorce he obviously wanted. Lists *always* help me think more clearly. This one let me see how much negative there was in our relationship, and how very little positive.

"Have we since divorced? Yes. We went to court the day after our ten-year anniversary, and the divorce was final three days later. Best thing I did. Worst thing was six months later: I let him move back in (still trying to save something that only existed in my mind!). That lasted about six months.

"Why did I send in my list? I heard about your collection and it simply intrigued me. These insights and secrets about people and their occasional idiosyncrasies are amazing. These lists were in a Franklin Planner that I no longer needed. Putting them to use instead of discarding them helped me to get rid of more garbage that I was toting around. Anything else I would like to add? I am done with men. No more. I figure I gave it a good try, and I'm just not interested anymore."

DIY LIST IDEA:
Behavior I Will No Longer Tolerate

What is wrong about my marriage
 drinking
 because 1) money 2) driving, 3) frequency,
 4) lateness, if at all, coming home
 5) atmosphere
 lying
 1) lying to me
 2) lying to me about being mugged
 3) other lies about where he was, how
 much money he has, etc.
 helping me with anything
 1) how much of a slob he is
 2) not picking anything up,
 3) not changing cat litter
 4) not doing dishes
 5) not doing laundry
 6) not doing anything for anyone but
 himself
Crappy Sex Life
 1) sleeping on the couch
 2) turning me down
 3) his actual body
 4) his lack of cleanliness
 5) his smell (alcohol, cigarettes, spices)
 6) grabbing me, taking his penis out
 7) lack of affection
Relationship with the kids
 1) way he treats   , especially
 2) poor example
 3) not playing sports, etc. not teaching
 them how to do anything
Relationship with me
 1) rarely talks to me about anything but
 himself
 2) never includes me in his activities —
 in fact seems to "exclude me" from
 most
 3) the lying, cheating, cover ups instead
 of honest communication
How little I respect him
 1) his inability to change or desire to try
 to change
 2) overall career record & earlier contributions
 3) his image to the community, my
 coworkers, his co-workers. Probably never
 change this.

There's a second side, too, if you can believe that. —S.C.

who: **STEPHANIE LIPECKY**

age: **34**

date: **MARCH 2004**

where: **AUGUSTA, GEORGIA**

"A mutual friend introduced me to Garret. At first I was hesitant about becoming involved, because he had a daughter, but after he made me laugh the first time, I was smitten. We hung out until 3 a.m. and went on our first date the following night. I remember the night we met vividly; seeing him for the first time and all our conversations. As quirky as I am, to find someone with such a similar personality and sense of humor is absolutely amazing! I don't know how Shannon knew that we would be such a match. Even three and a half years later we still thank her for introducing us every time we see her.

"I wrote this list before we were engaged but after we had moved in together. It was a one-year dating anniversary gift— something for him to keep forever, hence the neat penmanship. He proposed to me in August 2004, and we were married in April 2005. The love we share is different than either of us had ever felt before. Garret is the man of my dreams. We were completely blessed to have been introduced."

DIY LIST IDEA:
Little Things I Love About My Partner

Garret, I love...

Your always sunny disposition
Your selflessness
The way you always make everything seem OK
The way you believe in me
Your energy level
Your teeth
That you're so smart
The way you make me feel safe
Your Yankee accent
That you want to look good for me
The way you kiss me
Your spiky hair
Your organizational skills
The way you encourage me
When you whisper in my ear
That you're so funny
That you always wanna touch me
Your gorgeous body
The way you love my cats
When you talk about our future together
Your beautiful blue-green eyes
That you love to travel
The way you snuggle me at night
Your smooth skin
The way my heart skips a beat when a "394"
    number comes up on the caller ID

How you love me unconditionally
How sensitive you are
Always looking forward to tomorrow
The way everything you do, you make it
    seem like it's for me
That you have the biggest heart of anyone
    I know, and I'm truly blessed to have
    you in my life
The way I could go on and on, but can't
    due to lack of time

I think *I'm* in love with Garret. —*S.C.*

who: **GREG TYTHERLEIGH**

age: **32**

date: **SEPTEMBER 2006**

where: **LONDON**

A Husband's Ten Steps

"I saw an article about crap husbands and thought I wanted something to stop me from walking that path. With two young kids (one and two and a half), and my wife at home with them, it's all too easy to say, 'I'm the bread winner here—you run the house.' I don't want to be a Victorian husband who expects his dinner on the table every night with the kids quiet and the house spotless! So I wrote this list before things started getting to a hard place. I wrote it for my wife and me, so, yes, I showed it to her. Whilst she was pleased that I had written it, we agreed that acting upon it was what would make a real and lasting difference to our lives. Lists are only ink on paper—a series of ideas. What matters is action and making the list a reality. It's important that you understand this list was never written out of crisis. We have a great life together. I just wanted to make sure that I had something in place for the future, because I never want to lose what I have."

DIY LIST IDEA:
How I Can Be a Better Partner

: 10 WAYS TO BE A BETTER HUSBAND :

1. BE YOUR FRIEND - EXPRESS MY THOUGHTS AND FEELINGS
AND DON'T MAKE UNILATERAL DECISIONS WITHOUT TALKING TO YOU.

2. BE SELF-SUFFICIENT - YOU DON'T HAVE TO DO EVERYTHING FOR ME.
I WILL BOOK MY OWN DOCTORS & DENTISTS APPOINTMENTS!

3. BE PRODUCTIVE - IDENTIFY AND SHARE MY INTERESTS.
I WILL NOT BOUNCE FROM ONE BAD JOB TO ANOTHER → CAREER PLAN.

4. BE AN INVOLVED FATHER - I WILL TALK TO AND PLAY WITH
OUR CHILDREN EVERY DAY THAT I CAN - HELP WITH HOMEWORK,
PACK LUNCHES, VOLUNTEER AT SCHOOL FUNCTIONS.

5. BELIEVE IN RITUAL - I WILL TREAT CHRISTMAS, EASTER,
HALLOWEEN, PANCAKE DAY ETC AS IMPORTANT FAMILY TIMES.
I WILL PLAN BIRTHDAYS, WRAP PRESENTS, CHOOSE COSTUMES, PLAY GAMES.

6. BE YOUR LOVER - I WILL DRESS TO IMPRESS, PLAN SPECIAL DATES
AND PAY ATTENTION TO YOU.

7. BE A DOMESTIC GOD - SHOPPING, MEAL PLANNING, COOKING,
CLEANING. WORK TOGETHER ON HOME MAKING / DECORATING.

8. BE FINACIALLY RESPONSIBLE - PAY BILLS, PRIORITISE,
HELP TO MANAGE OUR MONEY. I WILL TALK ABOUT SPENDING / SAVING.

9. BE THE MAN I WANT TO BE - BE HONEST WITH MYSELF. I WILL
NOT BLAME OTHERS FOR ANY UNHAPPINESS. I WILL NOT SELF -
MEDICATE. I WILL CONFRONT ISSUES & SPIRITUALITY.

10. BE INSPIRATIONAL - I WILL BE SPONTANEOUS. I WILL
MAKE YOU LAUGH. I WILL **LOVE YOU** SO. XXX

Wives everywhere will show their husbands this list. —S.C.

who: **ZOE BURGESS**

age: **41**

date: **NOVEMBER 2000**

where: **HAYSVILLE, KANSAS**

Better off ALONE

"I wrote this pros-and-cons list back in November 2000, after dating this man for nine months. I was forty-one and had not been able to make a relationship work with a man for longer than four months since 1979. I became convinced that it was me (and not the men I was choosing). Although this relationship started out very magically, I stayed in it much longer than I wanted, trying to make it work. I met this fellow at a twelve-step group's Valentine's dance (thus, references to programs and sponsors). I finally could barely stand the sight of him and made this list to decide whether I should keep trying or start over. Once the list was created I saw plainly the imbalance.

"I ended the relationship before Christmas that year. He did not take it well, threatened suicide, called me, and left horribly hateful messages or deeply apologetic, loving messages about thirty to forty times a day. I finally spoke to him and told him, 'I am not responsible for your happiness.' I did not hear from him after that. I floundered for a while and made peace with the fact that I'd likely walk through this life alone. Because of this list, I knew I was better off, even alone, without him. In 2004 I met the man of my dreams and have been very happy with him for nearly three years now. This experience has reassured me that I needed to listen to my instincts and feelings all along. That in fact it was not me—it was the men. Ha!"

DIY LIST IDEA:
Times I Doubted My Instincts and
Shouldn't Have

Things I love

Likes to be busy
Very Generous
Listens
Doesn't Drink
Fixes things
Builds Things
Humble
Senses my Moods/Emotions
Compliments me
Lets me talk
Loves Children
is a little boy often
Is a Spiritual person
Is thin in shape
Very giving lover
makes me feel beautiful
makes me feel smart
Sponsors many guys
Has good friends

Things that Drive Me Crazy

stupid jokes - imagination
Reading of signs, Billboards, Movie titles, etc.
THE INCESSANT FLATULENCE!
Smells of Perspiration, (after a shower?)
Sneezes w/o Kleenex's
gets things out- leaves all over house
Doesn't like the window open
gets hair all over bathroom
Doesn't Love Charlie (cat)
Boasts of Ability to accomplish any
    Physical Feat ("I guarantee")
    Is Completely ignorant on Politics
Has great difficulty Communicating
CANNOT PUT (3) SENTENCES TO-
GETHER USING PROPER ENGLISH!!!
says Pol-ice, & I V
  Thinks an answer to Terrorism is to blow
    up The Great Pyramids,
  Decides he doesn't like a Restaurant if they
  don't have a smoking section
  Very inconsiderate, messy, smoker
  Never buys enough cigarettes for stay
    Always runs out
  Tells me derogatory things about most
  other people (especially guys) in Program
  Inept at talking on the phone
  Forgets things, many things
  goofiness is jerky & unattractive
Has virtually no relationship w/ children
and doesn't seem to want to pursue one.
  Is a High School Drop-out
  Has low self Esteem
  Can't kiss very well- especially during lovemaking
  Can't sing very well
Only other interest seems to be Program
Most annoying -clicking- sound w/ tongue
Cares for others more than himself
Bad sense of Humor
Is Not witty or clever
Jealous - Suspicious
  Suicidal on occasion

My fave: "Most annoying-clicking-sound w/ tongue." —S.C.

(The cons continue on p. 238)

TOPICS *to discuss with a* CRUSH

"I was drunk and wanted to call this guy. I was nervous about what to say. I'm pretty sure I never called, which is really good. I wrote this list while drinking. My handwriting gets progressively worse as I'm drinking, so if it's a long enough list, you can usually chart my evening. If I couldn't find someone to go drinking with, I would drink by myself and the lists would just pour out. For a while the other key drinking-alone activity was ordering shit from infomercials. I eventually started forcing myself to make lists of the things I wanted while drunk, to see if I still wanted them sober (never did)."

DIY LIST IDEA:
Things I Like to Do When I'm Drunk
(That I Don't Do Sober)

- Are you on your business trip
- Have you ever seen the movie Chaplain?
- " ~~business~~ " " w/ Keanu Reeves as
  a football player + ~~Gene Hackman~~ ~~man~~ as the
  coach? ~~What took you so long?~~ K: There was traffic.
- Or the one w/ Shelly Long as divorced writer (from a
  film maker) w/ young Drew Barrymore as child in the
  middle of it all? ~~Cindy from Brady Bunch~~ emotional monologue in court
- Or Julia Roberts as Daughter (another daughter
  is Lily Tomlin) of immigrants, working in a
  family-run pizza shop (Matt Damon + Vincent Onofrio
  also in it
- Also another one called 'Wishful Thinking' w/
  John Stewart
- These were all on tonight
  You don't treat a kid like your dog. That's it. (swelling,
  lesson-learning, family music)
- Do you like 'The Office'?
- Are you terrified of the movie Open Water?
- Will you read 'Everything is Illuminated'?
- Have you read A Confederacy of Dunces?

someone

Drunk dialing is always dangerous. Combine that with drunk listing and watch out. —S.C.

who: **BARB RIORDAN**

age: **35**

date: **2003**

A SOON-TO-BE DIVORCÉE TRIES TO MOVE ON

"I was getting divorced from my husband of two and a half years. Writing the list was part of my attempt to stop obsessing. You can see how effective it was! Did I succeed in throwing out all my underwear from the eighties and buying new black underwear? Yes, that was the fun and optimistic part! I figured divorcées had lots of black lace and I would get to use it."

DIY LIST IDEA:
My Qualities That Someone Else
Will Appreciate

Today

Have an A free day!
Call Carol's nice lawyer friend
Do Cindy, tape w/weights
What happened to David? Google him...
Vitamins
buy green tea
Meditate – no sleeping/crying!
Find tax returns
Don't think about A
Investigate women's therapy group
Call lawyer Dr. Chow recommended
Throw out all underwear from the 80's
use tanner
Banish A – no more
look up lawyer w/biggest ad in
                      yellow pages–fees?

Buy new underwear in <u>Black</u>

Be kind to myself and all others
                   (except A – I
                   hate him!)

What was she doing with underwear from the eighties in 2003? —S.C.

who: **A WOMAN in her first serious relationship with a woman**

age: **HER MID-TWENTIES**

date: **1995**

where: **PENNSYLVANIA**

Complicated Feelings

"Hate and like are intertwined, and you can't tell where one starts and one ends. I was feeling that way at the time. I had gotten into my first serious relationship with a woman. I felt like it was too much—too serious, too emotionally deep. She wanted this degree of intensity that men usually aren't interested in. But we were still best friends. I was confused. I hated her and loved her at the same time. I probably wrote at least fifty thousand words about this relationship in my journal. I would write about things obsessively trying to figure them out. How long did it last? It's really unclear because we were so nebulous. Maybe a year and a half but off and on.

"'Her car in front of my house': I was living with my parents for a while and she drove there and her car was in front of my house. I freaked out because my parents would see her. I was afraid she was going to tell my parents that I was a lesbian. She told me to trim my nails because she said all lesbians trim their nails, and I didn't know I had done this terrible thing by not trimming them. She was just crazy about dogs and I am not that into dogs. Just looking at this list I feel a sense of anxiety, still. I can still feel lust in this list, those shorts she wore that night we made love, yet there's a lot of annoyance also. The first line—I'm not talking to you, you think I'm talking to you but I'm not—it's almost schizophrenic, like she was inside my head."

> *DIY LIST IDEA:*
> *Things I Both Love and Hate*
> *About My Partner*

Obsessive List: 1995

I'm not talking to Libby
for a month Dec 12-Jan 12
take a break. I'm not talking to you
you think I'm talking to you, but I'm not

20 Things I like & hate
1. The way she's all over dogs
2. her voice
3. her hands
4. her lips feeling like cat kisses
5. her pimples
6. her staring at me across the room/boiler room?
7. her getting annoyed at something again
8. her car in front of my house
9. her getting annoyed at me
10. her jeans
11. those shorts she wore that night we made love
12. her hair
13. her career
14. talking about business
15. the old suitcase she carries shit in
16. the way she told me to trim my nails
17. her being so damn serious
18. that she thinks all my relations w/ men have been
horrible
19. her anger
20. missing her

Lesbian Rule 16: Trim your fingernails. —*S.C.*

"It's pretty DORKY
(and slutty too?)
that I kept a list of people
with whom I have slept.
I have a bad memory,
though,
and it would make me feel
even sluttier
to have
no idea who
or how many."

-for the full list and the
story behind it, turn to page 132

7 ~~Sex~~

People often have the notion that sex should be spontaneous. As if the sex was hotter in the first months of a relationship with zero planning. But in many ways that is a fiction. First dates, seductions, and petal-strewn bathtubs are all designed ahead of time. Like everything else, sex is more likely to happen if we push it to the front burner of the imagination, if we wear hotter underwear and plan for it. So it should come as no surprise that "sex" (sometimes with exclamation point!) should appear on so many to-do lists. My personal favorite directive is "get frisky." It sounds so playful, so energetic and open to interpretation, so much more fun than "fool around," "hump," or worst of all, "get nooky." It's fun to read "sex" in the midst of otherwise prosaic obligations like "printer paper." The mundane mixed with the erotic is in itself exciting.

Other lists go further than just listing sex as goal. The lists are reflections of our complicated relationship with sex itself—the thrill of exploring bondage and domination, fears about whether sex is worth all the anxiety it creates, and of course the iconic slept-with list, which has wide reverberations throughout pop culture. Who could forget the opening scene of the nineties film *Reality Bites*? Janeane Garofalo's character wakes up and pulls her diary out from her bedside table to note her sixty-sixth lover. She thinks hard before jotting down "Rick?" Got to love that question mark.

Most of our sex lists seem to be about quantifying our past. But my favorite sex lists tend to be about future planning. Somehow the dry, linear list nature contrasts well with the raciness of items on it. A friend showed me a hilarious sex list that, sadly, his date found too private to share here. He and his date got drunk, and my friend (always the list-maker) suggested they make a list of things they would like to do with each other sexually. They took turns passing a piece of paper back and forth. Number two is "sex in a field on an early autumn day," number seven is "me, you, and a tambourine," which my friend first thought was "me, you, and a trampoline." The items are hysterical, but the idea is sound. It's hard to tell someone places you like to be touched and things you like sexually when you're starting a relationship. Writing a list of things you like might be an easier way to communicate. Try it. The list does the initial talking. Then you can start crossing things off together.

who: **A YOUNG WOMAN who suffers from bipolar disorder**

age: **19 TO 25**

date: **STARTED THE LIST IN 1999, last entry in 2005**

Am I A Slut?

"It's pretty dorky (and slutty too?) that I kept a list of people with whom I have slept. I have a bad memory, though, and it would make me feel even sluttier to have no idea who or how many.

"What was the 'bad period of life'? That was my second bad depression, the period around guy number fifty with names missing. I cut myself off socially. I couldn't be around anyone in a normal sense. I went out alone with the intent of sleeping with someone. I had to be completely wasted.

"I'm pretty healthy now. I still drink, but I don't crave altered states. Even though it would sound better to say my improvements were due to personal strength, a large part has come from therapy and finally being properly medicated. (I'm rapid-cycling bipolar.) To give myself credit, the meds wouldn't work if I didn't take them religiously. I finally got to a place where I was tired of feeling out of control. Even the 'fun' parts of manic episodes became exhausting. Sometimes I can't shake the feeling that stability is boring, but I like where my life is now. I love being in love, that my boyfriend's my best friend, and that our relationship is stable. It's worth taking care of myself to keep things like that going."

DIY LIST IDEA:
People I've slept with

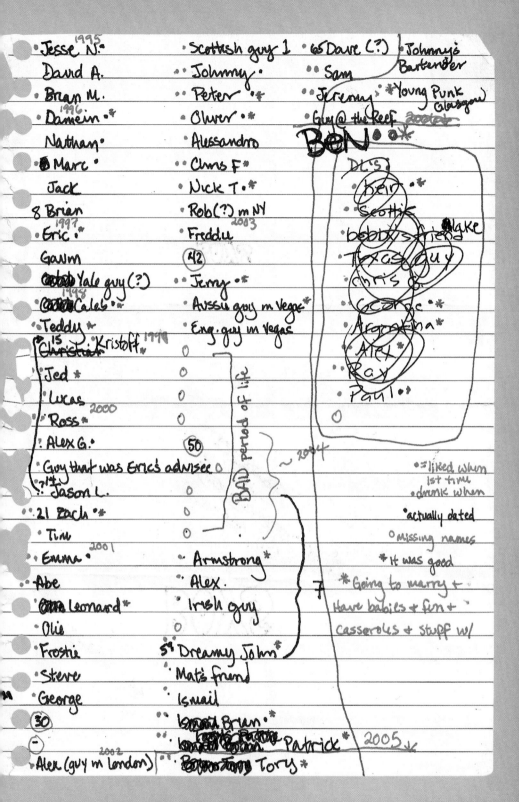

Hey, I slept with "Young Punk Glasgow" too! —S.C.

who: **SARAH ATLEE AND STEVEN (STEEV) T. CHARLESTON**

age: **22 AND 25**

date: **SUMMER 2003**

where: **ALBUQUERQUE**

twenty-something FRISKINESS

STEEV: "I wrote this list with Sarah, my girlfriend at the time. The memory is bittersweet. This woman with whom I had fallen so deeply in love had come back to town during a break in her studies. I had little else to focus on except my summer job (working at a cigar store) and my hobbies. These were languid, sun-washed days approaching her birthday, when I couldn't be around her enough before she flew away again."

SARAH: "We were buying earplugs for Steev's friends who had just moved in to a house together. I believe that earplugs help keep the peace between roommates, so it was my housewarming gift."

STEEV: "I can't recall this specific incident of friskiness, but it seems very likely that I was happy to cross it off my list. I had a desperate, rabid physical lust for this woman, partly because she was really, really hot, and partly because I knew in the back of my mind that it was all going to be taken away soon."

SARAH: "What he said."

DIY LIST IDEA:
Places Where I Would Like to Get Frisky

nux vomica

1. Sleep in a little
2. Steev visits bank
3. Steev gets Sarah
4. Visit Notary at Mail Bank
5. Go to Buffalo Exchange
6. Lunch @ Garcia's
7. Paintball Store - buy 3 bags *
8. Find Earplugs (smiths or walgreens) *
9. Make Spaghetti, Watch Flick
10. D&D

STAGS   P12
Pet food
homeop?
mail scrip, g. door opener

GO HOME
GET FRISKY

Nux Vomica = a homeopathic medicine Sarah needed to buy. —S.C.

who: **A YOUNG LESBIAN**

age: **21**

date: **NOVEMBER 2005**

where: **AUCKLAND, NEW ZEALAND**

KISSING HERSTORY

"At high school, everyone used to keep lists of guys they'd kissed. Although I kissed quite a few, I never got into those giggly conversations. After coming out as gay, I suddenly understood what it was like to have crushes and giggle about people you'd kissed. I wanted to remember each and every girl I kissed because it was so fantastic! This is what I'd been missing out on! Hence the list."

DIY LIST IDEA:
Most Memorable Kisses

Girls I've kissed:
Amy Nixon   2001
Amie   2003
Laura
Taylor   2004   American
Angelica   Mexican
Sandra
Jen
Jaime
Emma B.
Chick in Queenstown   English
Cathy (Laura again) 2005
(Sandra again)→Nadia
Monika   Polish
Penny
Ellen   2006
Lizzie
Petra   Croatian
Emily   April 2006

who: **KRISTI PAETZNICK**

age: **35**

date: **NOVEMBER 2005**

where: **ST. PAUL, MINNESOTA**

Exploring Bondage and Domination

"A friend suggested I start talking to this guy she knew. He wanted to explore the BDSM (Bondage, Discipline, Sadism, Masochism) lifestyle and I did, too. So I did some reading on the subject and met him. Great guy. Got him addicted to *Family Guy* and had bad sex once. Now we're just casual friends. Am I still interested in exploring BDSM? I might be if the right person came along. If I were to find someone who wanted to be in a monogamous, committed relationship and wanted to explore, then I'd probably go ahead and have it be another dimension to our sex life (although I haven't gone looking for other subs [submissives] to experiment with). Has anything happened on this front since writing this list? Nope. We talk occasionally but it's just normal conversation."

DIY LIST IDEA:
Sexual Things I'm Curious About Trying

Excitement?

Beginning to exchange e-mails with M — friend of M
He's a sub — aka a submissive.

1) Assertiveness a good thing.
2) Wonder if "Exit to Eden" is/would be helpful, educational?
3) Recommended Reading:
4) (If it involves getting massages I'm all for it.
5) So what does it really mean?
6) Am I expected to wear the "costumes" — some OK but the rest?
7) Only that "type" of sex?
8) Really need to learn more about this.
9) Can we "build" up to stuff.
10) ?
11) Should talk to M!
12) Wonder if he'll call tonight or this weekend? — Probably not, probably with the girlfriend. Its weekend after all
13) Will he break up with her? For me?
14) Will I want him? More than Bob?

Why is it that number 10 is the one I'm most interested in? —S.C.

who: **A WOMAN IN HER EARLY FORTIES**

when: **APRIL 2006**

where: **BOULDER**

to-do list for *bed*

"My boyfriend and I had been together a couple months. Our sex life was going well but like most of the men I've been with, he had a lot of questions. Where did I want to be touched, what did I want to do? I find it hard to answer questions like that in the moment. I decided it would be easier to write a list when I was alone and had time to think. He appreciated it. But by the time I gave it to him he had already discovered most of these things."

DIY LIST IDEA:
A Sexual To-Do List for My Partner

Things I like Sexually (an evolving list)

↳ you should
make me one

1. You massaging my scalp
2. You entering me from behind, I have <u>too</u> a vibrator in front
3. Caressing me everywhere
4. Going down on me, no pressure to come
5. Me kissing the sides of you
6. Me kissing your nipples
7. Fucking with one — clothes on
8. Your hand on my ass
9. Biting my ass, not hard, little pecks
10. Mild spanking while we are going at it, not sure how I feel about that
11. Biting my back up and down, my spine, lightly
12. One finger inside me while you go down on me
13. You rubbing my face, between my eyes, my temples
14. Little kisses everywhere

Who wouldn't want little kisses everywhere? —S.C.

who: **DUSTIN KIDD**

age: **HIS THIRTIETH BIRTHDAY**

date: **THANKSGIVING DAY 2005**

where: **A SOLO YOGA RETREAT**

sex—love it! ♡
BUT TERRIFIED OF IT

"I wrote this list in Costa Rica at a weeklong solo yoga retreat, my way of dealing with having just turned thirty. I was reading *If the Buddha Got Stuck* by Charlotte Kasl. These were the areas where I felt stuck. As for why I wrote that I'm terrified of sex, the older I get, and especially as I confirm that singleness is best for me (there's something deep in me that loves defining myself on my terms and not in conjunction with others), the more sex has become a source of anxiety. I have sex more often and better, but I worry that I'll cross a line one day where I'm too old to be successful in romance—and I'll never have sex again. It's irrational, I know, but it's a big worry. Sometimes I think life would be easier if I decided to be celibate. Then I wouldn't have to worry anymore, and I could feel that chastity was my choice and not a consequence of aging or romantic misfortune."

DIY LIST IDEA:
Ways I'm stuck Right Now

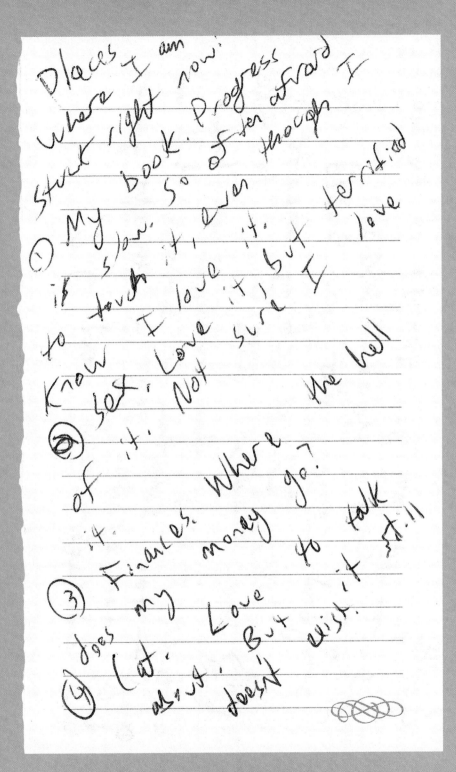

Places I am where I am stuck right now:

① My book. Progress so often slow, even though I love to touch it, even terrified. I know I love it, but I love it. Not sure I love it. Scared. Love it. Not sure of it.

② What the hell of it.

③ Finances. Where does my money go? Love to talk about it.

④ Cat. Love it. But it doesn't exist.

Talk about honest! —S.C.

who: **JAMYE WAXMAN**

age: **31**

date: **APRIL 2006**

where: **AT HER KITCHEN TABLE IN BROOKLYN**

ADULT MOVIE PROPS

"I was the producer and cowriter of *Under the Covers*, a comedy about women and their sex lives, and how what happens between the sheets isn't necessarily what we think it should be. It's part of a line of erotic films written and directed by a woman and from a woman's perspective. This was the prop list we sent to Femme Productions, the adult company financing the movie. The vibrators were used in a masturbation scene. (A sex toy clerk goes through many sex toys in order to deflower herself—her secret is, she's a virgin but nobody knows.)"

DIY LIST IDEA:
My Sexy Shopping List

CLOTHING REQUESTS
Fantasy Fishnet Chemise - Black/Small
Venus Babydoll - Blue/Small
ELEGANT BABYDOLL - Red/Small
Take the Plunge Chemise - Black/Fits All
Strappy Back Chemise - Black/Fits All
Sexy Lady Chemise - Black/Fits All
Secrets Chemise - Black/Fits All
Full Exposure Garter Set - Black/Fits All
Lace Tanga Shorts - Black/Med/Large
Lace Tanga Shorts - White/Small/Med
Sophisticated Lady Teddy - Black/Medium
Naughty Nightie - Blue/Small
HOT MAMA FENCE-NET TOP - Black/Fits All
Lady In Red Cami Set - Red/Fits All
Midnight Lace Pajamas - Black/Small
See-Through Boxer Brief - Black/Fits All
SEXY CATSUIT - Black/Fits All
You Give Me Butterflies Dress - Black/Fits All
Sheer Seduction Dress - Black/Fits All
Sexy Mini Dress - Lime Green/Fits All
Devil In The Red Dress - Red/Small
Fencenet Stocking w/Garter - Black/Fits All

SEX TOY STORE SCENE
Wascally Wabbit Vibrator - Wascally Wabbit
Product #: 2552-0000
Sheer Lady Finger - Green
Product #: 6855-5000
Rabbit iVibe - Pink
Product #: 7396-6200
Mini-Rabbit Rotating Vibe
Product #: 7972-0000
The Flicker Vibe
Product #: 5077-0000
I-Vibe Pocket Rocket - Blueberry
Product #: 4292-2300
I-Vibe Pocket Rocket - Strawberry
Product #: 4292-0200
Madame Butterfly Love Pillow
Product #: 7991-0000
Hitachi Wand Massager
Product #: 6550-0000
Fukuoku 9000 Massager - Fukuoku 9000
Product #: 3821-0000
Brown Sugar Cock
Product #: 7728-0000
Powder Blue Duo
Product #: 6432-0000
Duets Vibrator
Product #: 9594-0000
Vibrating Orgasm Balls
Product #: 8973-0000
Glow Worm Vibe
Product #: 1486-0000
Vibrating Erotic Symphony - Vibrating Symph
Anal Beadstick
Product #: 1294-0000
Carmen's 7" Fun Cock: LARGE - Carmen 7"
Fun Cock: Large
Product #: 6975-0000
6" Dong With Suction Cup
Product #: 1064-0000

A&E 5X Triple Pleaser - A&E 5X Triple Teaser
Product #: 8213-0000
Candy Cane Waterproof Vibrator
Product #: 6269-0000

FOR DUNGEON
Triple Thrillers Panty - Fits All
Product #: 2897-0095
Chain Front Teddy - Black/Fits All
Product #: 1764-8095
Bad Girl Collection
Product #: 7985-0000
A&E LOVE WHIP - A&E Love Whip
Product #: 5901-0000
A&E LOVE RESTRAINTS - A&E Love Ropes
Product #: 5911-0000
Leather Ring Harness
Product #: 6871-0000
Vibrating Strap-On Harness
Product #: 3270-0000
Weighted Nipple Clamps
Product #: 1447-0000
Erotic Nipple Chain
Product #: 4710-0000
Leather Love Bonds
Product #: 2163-0000
Universal Swing Stand
Product #: 2497-0000
Vibrating Heart Pleasure Harness - Vibrating
Heart Pleasure Harn.
Product #: 5417-0000
Tantalizing Teddy - Black/Fits All
Product #: 7742-8095
Beg Me Set - Black/Medium
Product #: 3366-8068
Love Bonds - Black Mink
Product #: 5719-9420

SAFER SEX
*** NEED TWO OF THESE
A&E Lube - Adam & Eve Lube
Product #: 5463-0000
***NEED TWO OF THESE
A&E SIGNATURE SILICONE LUBE - A&E
Signature Silicone Lube
Product #: 5813-0000
Super 100 Condom Sampler
Product #: 6403-0000

What do you keep in your dungeon? —*S.C.*

GLAZO-MANIA

n: An unusal passion for making lists.

8 OBSESSIVE-COMPULSIVE

"Obsessive" is a tricky word—what one person considers excessive another considers essential. Some people think making a list every day qualifies, which amuses me, because I think that writing a list every day is normal. For others, obsessive means waking up in the middle of the night in a panic to write a list; getting genuinely giddy at making lists; or reacting with apprehension if someone suggests an activity that wasn't part of today's plan.

All lists are a manifestation of our desire for control and organization, but obsessive lists reflect heightened desires. It's as if our insides are too disorderly, and it's only when everything is down on paper that we feel calm. The problems come when listing goes too far, and we start spending more time on the lists than doing anything on them. The *DSM-IV-TR*, the bible of mental disorders, includes list-making as one possible compulsion associated with Obsessive-Compulsive-Personality Disorder. My friend Hazel, whose list "Problems, Why Am I Not Pursuing Goals?" appears in this chapter, at one time might have qualified as "list OCD."

Hazel's family life was always chaotic. Her father was an alcoholic, and listing became a coping strategy. In her twenties, Hazel sometimes spent two or three hours a day making and recopying lists. The items on her lists were a constant jumble of concrete items like "buy mangoes" followed by conceptual to-dos like "become whole." She felt trapped by everything she wrote down—if it was on paper she had to live up to it. She had to quit listing for a few years. In her late thirties, she's become a more well-adjusted lister; she's no longer so attached to what she writes down. She loves writing grant applications for a nonprofit she started, because they include lists. She teaches life skills, including list-making, to women in prison.

On the opposite side of the spectrum are "done" listers, people who write down every single thing they do. Solomon Bernstein, whose hieroglyphic lists appear on page 149, spent his life noting almost all his tasks and possessions, stuffing those lists in his pockets, patting them habitually to make sure they were safe. Only after his father's death did his son Mashey examine the notes. Mashey speculates that listing, a habit that started in his father's childhood, might have been a way to bring more control to a life that at times seemed random. It might also have been a way to certify his existence. For "done" listers, like Solomon, there's a sense that nothing is real unless it's recorded.

who: **SOLOMON BERNSTEIN**

age: **88 TO 89**

date: **CIRCA 1995**

lists interpreted by: **HIS SON MASHEY**

A Rabbi's "Done" Lists

"For decades my father never changed his daily note-taking habit. He placed notes on the table, cut them up, and added new items. He then placed them in envelopes, which he put in his jacket pockets, patting them to make sure they were safe. On the first anniversary of his death, I lit a memorial candle and steeled myself to open envelopes sent home by the nurse. They were like ancient relics. All were written in his unmistakably beautiful penmanship, parts Hebrew, parts English. I realized he carried his whole life in his pockets.

"There were endless lists devoted to work at the synagogue where he was rabbi for more than sixty years: Hebrew names, anniversaries of deaths. The most typical dealt with his daily routine. A widower at eighty-seven, he spent his last three years living alone. He managed perfectly well, perhaps helped by notes. Everything was written down: 'face cloth,' 'hot water bottle,' 'teeth.'

"Last week, my uncle told me my father's habit began as a child. 'Went around the house with his little notebook, writing down things. We used to laugh at him.' Whether or not these notes gave a sense of control over things, I don't know. I only know these envelopes are now precious to me. When I finished reading them, I put them back in one of his jackets. Every so often I pat them to make sure they are safe."

> DIY LIST IDEA:
> Things I Don't Want to Forget
> About a Loved One

BEANS   ONION
GRAPEFRUIT. STRAWBERRIES
GRAPEFRUIT JUICE
CREAM. SOURED CREAM. RISODOL
FROSTIES. COFFEE. MELON
                    PEARS
P.G. GRANULES. INSTANT TEA. TEA.
SUGAR. CUBE SUGAR. CHEESE.
JAM. MILK. BUTTER. SALT.
7UP. SODA WATER.
HEINZ TOMATO KETCHUP
MACKEREL SARDINES
POTATOES. TIN SALMON.
        KIPPERS
HADDOCK. SALMON CUTLET
SMOKED IRISH SALMON
SMOKED TROUT. SOUP
CLOTHS. TOILET PAPER
KITCHEN FOIL KITCHEN TOWELS

DOCTOR HAIRCUT
WRITE P6437/c/
TEAR PAPERS
FIX P6437/c/ PAD
INCOME TAX
FLAT PAPERS
WEDDING ROSS REGISTERS
        REGISTERS
ALONY BOOK FILL IN NAME RABBI
QLONY   V. SILVERMAN

WRITE CASH PAPER DONE
WRITE P6437/c/ CARDS DONE
POST P6437/c/ CARDS DONE
PENCIL "SURNAME" DONE
WRITE OVER PENCIL 7/c/ DONE
    WORK P6437/c/
REGISTERS WEDDING
REGISTERS "NIL" GIVEN
FIX REGISTERS DONE
LOOK INTO RECEIPT DATE
REGISTERS CHECK QLONY √ DONE
NO REGISTER OF MARRIAGES
ALONY } IST BOOK NUMBERS 1-18 IN USE
ALONY } BOOKS BEFORE
MISSING REGISTER/S TORN √ DONE
REGISTERS BEFORE
    WILL √ DONE
INCOME TAX √ DONE
PAPERS FLAT √ DONE
        TEAR PAPERS

PACKING
-
SHOES. TIE. CHOCOLATES
SUIT. RAINCOAT
TABLETS NEW HAT
QUESTS ADJUR CANDLES
TISSUES CARDIGAN
6 HANDKERCHIEFS
SANDWICH 3 SOCKS
3 UNDER PANTS
4 SHIRTS DRESSING GOWN
7UP, AIDC, I UP
PHILISHAVE
JEWISH CHRONICLES
TAXI

COPIES FOR OLD REGISTER/S
    OLD FOR COPIES
COPIES FOR MY REGISTER/S
    MY FOR COPIES
COPIES FOR NEW REGISTER/S
    NEW FOR COPIES
COPIES FOR NEW NEW REGISTER/S
    NEW NEW FOR COPIES
OLD REGISTER/S TORN (COPY COPIES)

ALL MISTAKES ALL REGISTERS
& MAKE NEW OLD REGISTER/S
MAKE COPY FOR OLD REGISTER/S

For some people, lists are a legacy. —S.C.

who: **BELINDA**

age: **31**

dates: **2003**

where: **CAMBRIDGE, MASSACHUSETTS**

AN ACCOUNTANT'S grocery list

"I made the fresh-produce list when I decided to make a conscious effort to eat better. It was in my wallet for at least three or four years. Following it helped keep me from the temptation of buying sweets and junk food."

DIY LIST IDEA:
What's Always in My Refrigerator

FRESH PRODUCE - Best Buys

JANUARY – Apples, citrus; Broccoli, eggplant

FEBRUARY – Citrus, bananas, apples; Broccoli, spinach

MARCH – Citrus, bananas, apples; spinach, broccoli

APRIL – mushrooms, carrots, Bananas, citrus

MAY – Strawberries; Asparagus, spinach, tomatoes, cucumber

JUNE – Berries, citrus, nectarines; tomatoes, asparagus, cucumber, beans

JULY – Berries, pears, melons, peaches, plums, grapes; tomatoes, green beans, peppers, cucumber, potatoes

AUGUST – Grapes, peaches, melons, pears; beans, squash, carrots, eggplant, peppers, onions, tomatoes

SEPTEMBER – Apples, melons, pears, grapes; onions, ~~sweet potatoes~~, peppers, squash, tomatoes

Photocopy and carry in your wallet. —S.C.

who: **SARAHLYNN LESTER**

age: **30**

date: **SEPTEMBER 2005**

where: **KIRKWOOD, MISSOURI**

Mickey Mouse Spreadsheet

"This is one page from a six-page grid for my family's trip to Walt Disney World. I included travel itineraries, flight numbers, meal plans with confirmation numbers, and attractions we wanted to see at each theme park, as well as shops and parades. I made copies for my husband and myself, put them in plastic sleeves to avoid water damage, and attached one to our stroller.

"What inspired me to make our itinerary so detailed? I'd like to say something significant, like 'I was having trouble dealing with parenting a two-year-old child with special needs (my daughter has Down Syndrome), and making detailed lists helps me feel like I have more control over my life.' Perhaps that's true. But the first truth is that I enjoy making lists; I enjoy being prepared, and it made the whole vacation very low stress. (We didn't stick to the itinerary, but we always knew what our options were!)

"Do I consider myself an organized person? No! But I can't remember not making lists. I carry a notebook with me at all times (and have for years). When I can't sleep at night, I turn on the light and make lists of things I need to do, buy, call, think about until I'm relaxed enough to go to sleep."

DIY LIST IDEA:
Most Memorable Vacations

Lester-Boal Walt Disney World Vacation 2005

Date	Location	Activities	Meals	Other
Thursday, September 22	Sarahlynn and Ellie travel to WDW	Paul, Sarahlynn, and Ellie converge upon Coronado Springs Resort and meet in the lobby.	Lunch in the Pepper Market	American Airlines 1098 7:14 AM Arrive: Orlando 10:32 AM Seats: 9E, 9F
	Fort Wilderness Resort & Campground: Tri-Circle-D Ranch & Farm		Dinner at Liberty Tree Tavern in Liberty Square in The Magic Kingdom. Priority Seating: 6:35 pm 36243914	Disney's Coronado Springs Resort Water View Rom Non-smoking, crib, refrigerator Confirmation: 65497071
	The Magic Kingdom (open 9 am – 9 pm)	Lunch, then nap as needed/possible Travel by taxi to Fort Wilderness for pony ride		Pony rides – No reservations necessary: 10 am – 5:00 pm daily. Parent can walk with child. $3.00 + tax this is their quiet time of year
		Boat to The Magic Kingdom. Visit Mickey's Toontown Fair and have dinner.		
		SpectroMagic Parade 8:00 PM 9/22, 24		
		Wishes: 9:00 PM 9/22, 24; 8:00 9/23, 25		

Who needs spontaneity when you have Excel? —*S.C.*

who: **HAZEL**

age: **IN HER TWENTIES**

date: **CIRCA 1994**

where: **AT THE LIBRARY**

A RECOVERING LIST OBSESSIVE

"I imagine this list was an answer to other lists that I wrote with big goals: get land, get a job, get out of the system. My other lists were pretty visionary, but in my twenties I was really existing on a day-to-day-survival level and wasn't able to take on those bigger goals. I guess I was depressed. I was trying to be specific with constructive criticism. But if you are just surviving, there is no balance between long- and short-term goals.

"In 2000, I decided: enough with this listing. I needed to quit for a while. I still like to write things down. But now I'm not as attached to the actual list. Being attached to the list can be a real problem. I really think it was obsessive. I would spend a lot of time rewriting lists and looking at them. This was in the early nineties, before people had laptops. It just took a lot of time. A list three pages long could take an hour to rewrite. I definitely had ideas of how I should be, and if I wrote it down, I would have to attend to it. The list took on a life of its own. Now I guess I'm more accepting that there's this part of me that wants to be all perfect, but I just can't do that for you, list."

DIY LIST IDEA:
Goals I Would Like to Pursue
(but I'm Not)

PROBLEMS [WHY AM I NOT PURSUING GOALS]

- SCHEDULE
- MOTIVATION
- LACK OF CONCENTRATION
- MISUSE OF TIME
- UNDEFINED OBJECTIVES
- NEED TO FOCUS
- RISKS UNKNOWN
- FEAR OF FAILURE
- NEED TO START FROM SCRATCH
- GET ORGANIZED
- ACT ON IDEAS
- DOMESTIC SITUATION
- PERSONALITY FLAWS
- INDECISIVE
- NEED COHERENT PLAN
- NO BALANCE BETWEEN LONG AND SHORT TERM

When you're writing lists in response to other lists, it might be time to take a break. —S.C.

who: **BEN CARPENTER**

age: **28**

date: **SEPTEMBER 2006**

where: **SAN FRANCISCO**

Get Up/Go to Sleep

"I write 'get up' on my list almost every day. I'm not sure when it started, but the lists began in college. Getting up is a big deal. If I don't do it in time, the day is shot. Besides, it gives me a guaranteed check."

DIY LIST IDEA:
My "I Know I Can Do This Today" List

Ask for Anotr
Copy of (B tu Bk)

Tuesday

Get Images
of CAT in yard

New Shop Images
- welders
- welding Helmets
- SWARF & tools
- chasing tools

~~Get up~~
~~Pack yoga clothes / Rice~~
~~Drive to work~~
~~Make food / Tea~~
Top Rails
~~CALL Dey / Set up meeting~~
~~Lunch~~ : ~~Veggies~~
~~Get notebooks~~
~~Get timer~~

Punch out
Bike to YMCA
~~Yoga~~
~~Sleep~~
~~Oregon~~
Ticket

CALL
Lil

Lil is Ben's grandmother. He calls her every week. —*S.C.*

who: **A WOMAN about to leave on vacation**

age: **35**

date: **AUGUST 2005**

RUDIMENTARY TASKS

"It's not that I can't remember to brush my teeth or take a shower or dress. It's that I get flustered and have overly high expectations for what I should be able to accomplish in an hour. Writing everything down helps me to set appropriate expectations. It helps me remember that every little thing takes time. There's a calm and orderly feeling, as if the list is looking over me. Sometimes it does feel obsessive, like, why can't I just float through life doing the things I need to do without writing them down first; but other times, it feels like nothing will happen unless it's written down."

DIY LIST IDEA:
What Always Needs to Happen Before
Leaving on Vacation

Wash dishes
floor
~~brush teeth~~

~~pack clothes~~
~~vitamins~~ →
~~food~~

~~shower then~~

Lucky for her she crossed off "dress." —*S.C.*

who: **CHRIS THOMAS**

age: **27**

date: **AUGUST 2002**

where: **BROOKLYN**

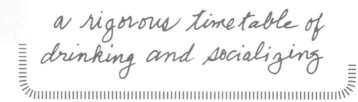

a rigorous timetable of drinking and socializing

"For most of my life I scheduled every day by the hour or half hour. But that's not as Type A as it sounds, since my schedules often included things like '3 p.m.–5 p.m. hang out,' '5 p.m.–6 p.m. have coffee.' My favorite on this particular schedule is '10–11 drink' then '12–1/2 Spa' (a nightclub). That's like fastidiously scheduling 'drinking beer' for one hour, then 'drinking vodka' for the next two hours."

DIY LIST IDEA:
Drinks I Like

3^{15}-3^{45} buy phone (rug?)
4- gym
    shower
5 Sasha arrives
6^{15} leave for movie
7-9 Public Housing
9-10 look at photos
10-11 drink
12-1/2 Spa

What happened between eleven and twelve? —*S.C.*

who: **JENNIFER WELLS**

age: **33**

date: **OCTOBER 16, 2006**

where: **EAST LANSING, MICHIGAN**

BipoLar Mood Chart

"I was in the middle of a bipolar episode where I was feeling happy, sad, angry, calm, irritable, agitated, and anxious—all in the span of two hours. I designed the chart to try to gain some sense of control. It obviously bothers me that my moods fluctuate so often. But the chart is fantastic. All I have to do is make an X. It did help me feel calmer and less afraid.

"I recently made a year's worth of charts and put them in a binder so that I can better understand this diagnosis and monitor my moods. It helps me to see what is going on with me in a way that I can't deny. I'm also including my writing, journaling, and blog posts according to the week they are written. It's a documentation of my life. I put a title page at the front of the binder that says, A Year in the Life of Me: Grad School, Motherhood, and Bipolar NOS (Not Otherwise Specified). Would I consider myself an obsessive list-maker? Mmm. Yes. I'm also a doctoral student in a field that assists people with mental illness. It's weird to be on both sides."

DIY LIST IDEA:
A Single Day's Moods and What
Triggered Them

Mood Tracking Chart

	MONDAY 10.16	TUESDAY 10.17	WEDNESDAY 10.18	THURSDAY 10.19	FRIDAY 10.20	SATURDAY 10.21	SUNDAY 10.22
GOOD							
SLEEP							
GOOD							
SLEEP BUT GROGGY						X	X
CALM							X
LIFE IS GOOD						X	
LIFE SUCKS		X	X X	X		X	
THINGS SEEM TOO LOUD IRRITABLE							
ANXIOUS		X				X X	
CRYING/SOBBING/WEEPY		X		X	X	X	
ANGRY, ANGRY, ANGRY		X					
CARE/DON'T CARE *BOTH 10/20*	X	X					X
TOO TIRED	X						
YELLING, LOUD	X						
IRRITABLE, CALM, IRRITABLE, CALM		X				X	X
ANXIOUS IN MY CHEST, MY SKIN, MY		X					
BODY, ANXIOUS EVERYTHING	X						
ANXIOUS IRRITABLE, MAD					X	X	X
HAPPY, HAPPINESS							∿∿∿∿∿
TOO LOUD, ALMOST YELLING	X	X	X				
DON'T WANT TO MONITOR MY							
MOODS, DON'T WANT TO DEAL							
DON'T WANT TO MOVE, OR MONITOR							
MY MOODS, OR ANYTHING				X			
HEAD TALK, NON-STOP CHATTERING.		X		X	X	X	
MEAN THING SAID. STOP. STOP. STOP.							
I CAN SEE THE POINT IN ALL OF THIS							
LIVING STUFF.							
OTHER.					X	X	X
COMMENTS		BUS DRIVER MAD AT ME B/C I JAMMED MACHINE w/CHANGE. SCREWED UP MIDS	TALKED TO PROF. ABOUT MED. TERM/ DIAGNOSIS			A LITTLE ON AND OFF	X

DETACHED

TERM. SOBBING. BLA

Comments labels: ENERGY! UP LATE. — IRRITABLE, MAD OR DEPRESSION

Annotations:
- Depression after 3 PM. AM better, steady and calm. ✗
- ENERGY! PM - up late
- * Afraid of how I might behave at party w/ friends. Afraid of how I would be w/ people.
- FREAKED OUT IN LAUNDRY - PARANOID? AGITATED

* I have been very anxious and very irritable/angry all week ((or 6/7 days). Quick temper. Loud voice. Feel mean. Not much patience.

FORGETFUL

Here's to more Sundays in Jennifer's life. —S.C.

who: **MARY TEAGUE COLLINS and her**
mother-in-law, Marge Collins

date: **SEPTEMBER 2004**

where: **WAITING FOR A PLANE AT LAX**

for: **MARY'S DAUGHTER MEGAN**

Thanksgiving Plan

MARY: "Who is Martha and why did we 'axe' her? Martha Stewart, and we axed her for being too complicated, fussy, and expensive in her ideas. She is kind of a joke in our house, and my mother-in-law, Marge, doesn't like her, period! I wouldn't consider this list so much obsessive as complete. But my children and most of humanity probably would."

MEGAN: "Yes, my mother does make obsessive lists, but they make my life easier, so why would I complain? I think the chart helped me to enjoy the holiday more, because I didn't have to plan anything out myself. It was all right there for me from the very beginning."

DIY LIST IDEA:
Our Thanksgiving Family Food Traditions

	A	B	C	D

Thanksgiving Planner according to Martha (Grandma and I axed her, except for the Turkey tecnique. Her stuff is just to Fussy), Marge and Mary

Finished	Task	When	Comments
	Plan Menu - Separate Worksheet	Mid November	The earlier you plan the sooner you can start buying, this stuff costs a small fortune!
	Tableware	Early November	Do you have enough, plates, silverware, glasses, napkins etc. If not, try the Dollar stores or Walmart, they have decent plates for .97. Since you have children, expensive dinnerware is just silly. Also, don't set the table until just before dinner or you'll be chasing toddlers to retreive you tableware!
	Cooking equipment	October or early November	Meat Thermometer, large roasting pan, crock pot, 8 qt stock pot, 9x13 pan, Pie tins (or buy frozen dough in the tins),
	Center piece	Mid November	Not a necessity, but a really nice touch. Candles by themselves are always a classic.
	Deep clean	Mid November	Deep clean the bathrooms, prepare linens for guest & clear out the refrigerator.
	Make shopping list	Mid November	"Make a list and check it twice" --Kris Kringle
	Shop	Mid November & 2 days before	Buy non-perishables early and shop for perishables a couple of days before Thanksgiving. Under no circumstances walk into a retail or grocery store the day before Thanksgiving. It just isn't good time management.
	Pre-cook 1	Two Days before	Make Cranberry Relish
	Pre-cook 2	Night before Thanksgiving	Pies, Sweet Potatoes, Potatoes, Stuffing
	Order Pies from Marie Calendars	1 week ahead	Choose Thanksgiving Day pickup.
	Thanksgiving Day cooking	Thanksgiving Day	For Dinner at 5pm (with a 18 pound Turkey): Have a leisurely breakfast because the work doesn't start until 10am if you pre-cooked the night before. See time line below.

Time	Task		
9:00 AM	Somebody pick up pies		
10:00 AM	Prep the Turkey and Baisting Sauce		
10:30 AM	Turkey goes in the oven		
12:00 PM	Start Bread dough for rolls if homemade		
1:30 PM	Start veg side dishes/but don't cook until 4pm	Keep baisting that Turkey	
2:00 PM	Punch down dough and shape for second rise		
3:00 PM	set the table		
4:00 PM	Cook sides		
4:30 PM	Turkey out of oven to rest. Make Gravy and put the Rolls (cook) and stuffing (reheat) in the oven		
4:45 PM	Have everyone help carry stuff to the table.		
5:00 PM	Give thanks to Heavenly Father and enjoy the fine dinner you made and the family who loves you.		

No matter what happens this holiday season, keep basting that turkey! —*S.C.*

1. diets I've been on 2. Spa treatments I would enjoy 3. things that give me energy 4. things that drain my energy 5. things I do when I have a cold 6. Ways I deal with insomnia 7. things that are good for my mental health 8. Signs I'm burned out 9. Things that make me sick 10. Good experiences with doctors 11. Bad experiences with doctors 12. Worst dental moments 13. Foods that make me feel alive 14. Unhealthy indulgences I permit myself 15. Health tips I've learned the hard way 16. Things I eat when stressed 17. New ways to exercise 18. Reasons to get healthy 19. Best DVDs to watch when sick 20. ways to cope with anxiety

9 HEALTH and SICKNESS

These health lists might be my favorites in the collection, or at least the most compelling. That might seem odd, because some *are* depressing—a young woman deals with a painful urinary tract infection; a schoolteacher lists twenty-eight reasons for losing weight, to "make Mom happy," "avoid insurance hassles," and "stop eliciting sympathy." Maybe it's just an expression of schadenfreude—the enjoyment of other people's problems—but, actually, I think their appeal is not that simple.

There's something very powerful about these health lists. They represent the moment when a person took control, when he or she stopped looking to doctors, the Internet, and experts for answers and wrote the prescription him- or herself. A depressed woman puts on her "to-don't" list: don't "stay in bed, indulge yourself, use the Internet for bullshit, be a victim." A recovering alcoholic writes himself a prescription of "no cigarettes," "exercise," "breathe . . . ," and "therapy."

Even after reading these health lists many times, I find them arresting. There's a degree of urgency in them that is hard to ignore. The emotional state in which they were written still seems to radiate from the page. "Points to Ponder" is crinkled from being written more than ten years ago, but still has a feeling of both clarity and desperation in it. The twenty-four-year-old man who wrote it was coming to terms with being on kidney dialysis and diagnosed as legally blind, which meant he would never be able to fulfill his lifelong dream of flying a plane. Even the headline, written at an angle, feels influenced by his state: It looks like an airplane trying to take off.

I've also included lists written by people struggling with depression. Lists make us feel in control, and feelings of control—whether real or illusory—are essential to mental health. That's why therapists often recommend lists to their clients. At the same time, anyone who has experienced depression knows that thoughts in this state are often marked by severe self-judgment. "Bad Habits" reflects that state: A woman was so convinced that her most innocent bad habits ("tuning out during office meetings" and "obsessive checking of email at work") were signs there was something wrong with her. She compared writing the list to "popping a pimple." At least then the thoughts were outside of her, and she could quantify the problem of her self-criticism on the page.

who: **A RECOVERING ALCOHOLIC**
and drug abuser

age: **HIS LATE THIRTIES**

date: **MARCH 2006**

Unfathomable SORROW

"I found this list on my friend M's desk. The thing that caught my eye was 'unfathomable sorrow.' I can see where quitting smoking would be hard, but I thought that was a bit hyperbolic. I mentioned this to M and we both chuckled over it—but then he remembered why he wrote it. His Mom died of lung cancer a couple of years ago, and this is what 'unfathomable sorrow' referred to."

DIY LIST IDEA:
Things I've Given Up to Be Healthy

LIFE!!

- NO CIGARETTES (unfathomable sorrow)
- Exercise
- Vitamin 2x
- Herbs 3x
- AA 2-3x a week
- Breathe . . . .
- limit Caffeine
- Accupunchure
- Limit nicotine tablets
- therapy 1X
- massage (every other week)

Hey, why not a massage *every* week? —S.C.

who: **TRISHA WHITE PRIEBE**

where: **FORT PIERCE, FLORIDA**

job: **SCHOOLTEACHER**

goal: **TO LOSE NINETY-TWO POUNDS**

A TEACHER SIGNS UP FOR WEIGHT WATCHERS

"I wrote this list at my desk after a long day of teaching. Obviously I am overweight, and I struggle with the motivation to fight obesity. I have tried relentlessly to lose weight. I do better with my reasons in front of me. I can't think, 'Wow! This weight will never come off!' Instead I must focus on the list. My top three reasons are to have healthy babies, to stop eliciting sympathy, and to have and enjoy my future. Since writing it, I joined Weight Watchers with a friend and we are losing, slowly but surely."

DIY LIST IDEA:
Ways I Could Be Healthier

REASONS FOR LOSING WEIGHT:

1. to increase my energy
2. to reduce my stress level
3. to feel fabulous
4. to avoid thinking people are laughing at me
5. to be able to buy cute clothes
6. to make Mom happy
7. to quit avoiding events like reunions
8. to look good in a tee-shirt
9. to reduce the fear of rejection
10. to not take "fat jokes" personally
11. to have healthy babies
12. to avoid insurance hassles
13. to wear anything in my closet
14. to help avoid cancer
15. to fight heart disease
16. to impress my husband
17. to find confidence
18. to wear a normal bathing suit
19. to stop feeling achy
20. to weigh less than TV people's "Before" pictures
21. to quit considering food the "enemy"
22. to stop avoiding mirrors
23. to stop eliciting sympathy
24. to enjoy - not avoid - cameras
25. to set a good example for children
26. to embrace public speaking
27. to stop the negative self-talk
28. to have and enjoy my future

Penmanship alone was reason enough to include this list. —S.C.

who: **LAURA ANGELL**

age: **HER MID-THIRTIES**

date: **CIRCA 2004**

why so miserable?: **A URINARY TRACT INFECTION**

uninsured and SICK

"I had a urinary infection and didn't have health insurance. I had nowhere to go. I went to a health clinic that is basically for homeless people. The man there was mean to me. I just felt like his questions suggested it was my fault or I would get over it eventually. Sometimes I have nightmares and fears about my health, and I guess I was having nightmares. I don't know why it says 'Mad Dog.' I almost feel like I was the mad dog. [Laughs.] It's a list of the five most miserable things, but I only have four. I do this often. When I make lists I want to have a solid number, so I make the numbers first, and then somehow I peter out before I get to the final number."

DIY LIST IDEA:
Five Worst Things That Happened
to Me This Week

5 Most Miserable
Things This
Week
1. Man at Tom Wadell
Clinic
2. Night nausea/burning
urine
3. Nightmares/paranoid
health fantasies
4. Mad Dog
5.

Thank God there was no number 5. —S.C.

who: **AN ACADEMIC with an alcohol problem**

age: **MID-THIRTIES**

date: **SUMMER 2006**

where: **NEW YORK CITY**

DRINKING vs. RUNNING

"I was clearly drinking way too much, especially given all of the other things I was trying to do—teach, write a book, and run a marathon—but in no way was I ready to quit drinking altogether. So I started seeing a cognitive behavioral therapist, who tried to help me to better manage my drinking. She told me to keep a journal in which I was to decide, each morning, whether or not I would drink that day and, if so, how many drinks I would allocate for myself. Just before bed each night, I was supposed to write down how many drinks I'd actually had. Obviously, the two columns were supposed to be identical. (The inclusion of daily exercise on the right side of the page was my own innovation.)

"When I first started the experiment, I was kind of excited! I didn't mind telling my friends what I was doing, and I was pleased with myself for being successful with this new strategy. But as soon as the plan started unraveling—which, I admit, didn't take so long—I hated that fucking list."

DIY LIST IDEA:
My Exercise/Drinking Diary

June 27	0	0	gym
June 28	0	0	2 miles
June 29	2	2	gym
June 30	4	4	7 miles, gym
July 1	4	4	
July 2	0	0	6 miles
July 3	4	5.5	5 miles
July 4	2	2	
July 5	0	0	
July 6	0	0	5.5 miles, gym
July 7	4	7	6 miles, gym
July 8	4	7	
July 9	0	9	
July 10	0	0	
July 11	0,	0	gym
July 12	0	0	gym 6 miles
July 13	2	2	gym
July 14	4	9	6 miles, gym
July 15	4	12	
July 16	0	0	
July 17	0	0	gym
July 18	0	0	3 miles

July 19	4	6	5 miles/gym
July 20	0	0	6 miles
July 21	3	6	gym
July 22	0	6	TIME TO GET
July 23	0	6	SERIOUS AGAIN
July 24	0	3	6.5 miles
July 25	1	1	gym
July 26	3	4	5.5 miles/gym
July 27	0		4 miles/gym

My advice would be to always stay in and read on July 15. —S.C.

who: **EMILY AC**

age: **24**

date: **MAY 2006**

where: **BOSTON**

Keeping Slow and Lingering Death in Perspective

"As I get older and doctor visits get more cursory (yet more things are achy), I have to make a list; otherwise I get flustered and forget to ask about things that are bothering me. The lists do help, even if they are depressing to make. Did I get these things checked out? I did! I had an appointment with a new doctor who was so nice and helpful. She told me that 75 percent of people who have migraines can bypass all the pain, devastation, and vomiting if they take a massive dose of ibuprofen as soon as they feel a trigger, which for me is my eyeball—it would swell lightly. It worked! I haven't had a migraine since. Why did I write such a serious list on such comical paper? I'm kind of a random and excitable person, and I love that paper so much! I only use it for lists that will be important; otherwise I just use old daily Sudoku papers, which are smaller and I often lose. I guess I like to temper my hypochondriacal nature by trying not to take things as seriously as I in fact feel they are. The pineapple baby helped me keep slow and lingering death in perspective."

DIY LIST IDEA:
Things to Get Checked Out at the Doctor

Things That Bear
Checking Out

1. migraines that end in
vomiting, warning &
recovery (eyeball)
2. bump on right leg
4-15
3. swollen ankles (random)
4. strained elbow
5. ~~excema~~ ~~excema~~
excema on fingers

I want a pineapple-baby notepad. —S.C.

who: **JAMES NEUBAUER**

age: **24**

date: **1995**

where: **ONTARIO, CANADA**

still alive and
ABLE TO WRITE A LIST

"I wrote this list during a dark time. I was on kidney dialysis and my girlfriend at the time broke up with me because she did not want to be a live-in nurse. Around the same time, the optometrist told me that my eye condition (a fairly rare astigmatism) could not be corrected through surgery, thus dashing forever my hopes of flying a plane. When I was told, I was very upset and smashed all my airplane models.

"Luckily my brother John gave me one of his kidneys and I am doing great now. I still thank my brother every time I see him, sometimes jokingly, like, You do not have to get me any birthday/Christmas gifts, *ever*. I do remember writing my list 'points to ponder.' It gave me some focus and helped me to remember the fact that at least I am still here, still alive, and able to write a list. It made me glad to have family and move on in a positive way. I saw many people die on dialysis."

DIY LIST IDEA:
Ways Family Members Have Been
There for Me

Points to PONDER

— Realize that I can never be
a pilot.
— Stop dwelling on the fact that I
am legally blind. — Yes many doors are
shut to me! but I have to stay positive.
— Never forget to always thank my brother
for giving me a kidney - and saving
my life. (I love my brother)
— Thank my whole family for being there for
me, → Mom + Dad, sister, Bro.

I love his brother too. —S.C.

who: **A RECENT COLLEGE GRADUATE**

age: **23**

date: **JANUARY 2003**

where: **NORTHAMPTON, MASSACHUSETTS**

To-Do List of a New Englander with Seasonal Affective Disorder

"I wrote this list in January 2003 in a $212/month apartment. I shared the house with a thirty-eight-year-old elevator operator who looked like Jesus and always wore his bathrobe, and a genius carpenter who dropped out of Villanova during his last semester because he couldn't think of anything he wanted to do with his degree. I had graduated from college and was having a *lot* of trouble adjusting. I had worked so hard—I read ancient Greek, for cripes sakes—and thought the world would see me coming. It didn't. Not even close. I was broke. I knew I wanted to be a writer, but I didn't yet have the guts or life experience to actually do it.

"I wrote 'Use your light therapy!!' because I have seasonal affective disorder. It's always worse when my life isn't going well. It's one of the reasons why I went to Africa in the Peace Corps (yes, I did go), but not until September 2004. Africa is sunny, and I always get a springtime urge to migrate.

"Do the different colors have any significance? I didn't think so, but now that I look at the list, I see that the green ink is a totally different voice than the blue—my positive alter ego encouraging the more rooted depressed one, although I wasn't conscious of that. Using different colors and voices is not something I normally do. Given the difficulty of my life at that time, I think the green was a much-needed seed of hope inside of me—the part of me that wanted to live."

> **DIY LIST IDEA:**
> **Things I Definitely Should Not Do**
> **When Depressed**

To Do	To Don't
· get up ▼▼ !!	· Stay in bed
· Use your light therapy▼▼!!	· indulge yourself
· call the bank - see if you	· use the internet
have enuf $ for gas.	for bullshit
· call Melissa - you blew	· be a victim
her off last week - you	
need to send your	
peace corps application in	

· get up ▼▼ !!
· Use your light therapy▼▼!!
· call the bank - see if you
  have enuf $ for gas.
· call Melissa - you blew
  her off last week - you
  need to send your
  peace corps application in
  yes, I relish challenge. I got
  out of bed today. Send me
  to Africa!
· ~~look for Social Security card~~
· call Aaron. you blew him off too
  he probably wants his money
· send your resume to the
  Food Bank Farm - you blew that job off. It's
    probably too late (as usual) but do it anyway.
· ~~clean out email box~~
· call verizon for another phone line
· call Lynn. You blew her off too.
· print out a resume
· Shower ▼
· clean out car
· try to sell some books
· think about prostitution or being a bike
  messenger. you're young, creative, healthy.
    USE it GIRL!! You can make bank and have
    Sex. OR Ride your bike. develop a business
    plan.
· ~~rewrite resume~~
· hike, call Jenny
· class at 4¹⁵

To Don't
· Stay in bed
· indulge yourself
· use the internet
  for bullshit
· be a victim

In   noho
· SS card
· temp agency
· lu 4¹⁵

Make bank *and* have sex: not a bad plan. —S.C.

who: ANOTHER DEPRESSED YOUNG WOMAN

age: 30

date: SPRING 2004

where: SAN FRANCISCO

NEGATIVE self-talk

"I wrote this list one Saturday afternoon in the spring, when it was beautiful outside and I was really depressed. I was sitting alone in my studio apartment feeling very isolated. It's disturbing that I could think of this many bad habits about myself. I guess I thought of them more as flaws, signs that there was really something wrong with me. But so many of these are common. 'Don't have mental energy/curiosity to follow most foreign news or even complex domestic stories.' Who does? It's funny that I was mad at myself for hiring someone to clean twice, but at the same time, I was upset that I 'hate washing dishes, and often let them sit 2, 3, 4, 5 days.'

"I actually brought this list to a therapy session to try to figure out why I am walking around thinking there is something wrong with me. The therapist pointed out that none of the individual items on this list were so bad, but what was sad was that I thought they were. Writing the list was helpful, though. It gave me a picture of this mess in my head and helped discharge all those bad thoughts. It was kind of like popping a pimple. At least the thoughts were outside me."

DIY LIST IDEA:
Things I Should Stop
Beating Myself Up About

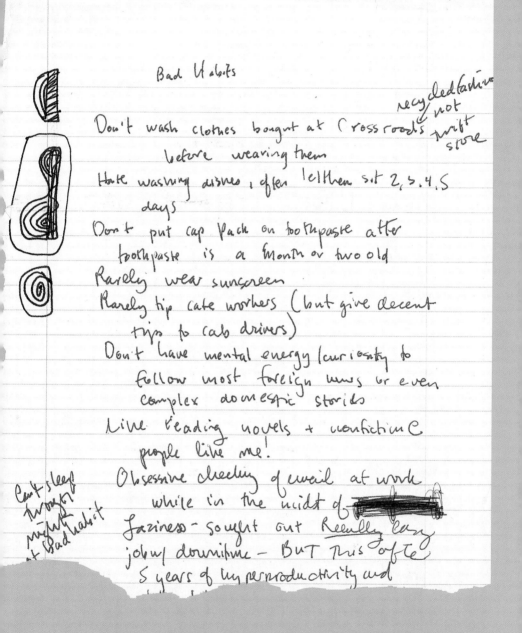

Bad Habits

Don't wash clothes bought at Crossroads ~recycled fashion not~ thrift store before wearing them

Hate washing dishes, often let them sit 2, 3, 4, 5 days

Don't put cap back on toothpaste after toothpaste is a month or two old

Rarely wear sunscreen

Rarely tip cafe workers (but give decent tips to cab drivers)

Don't have mental energy/curiosity to follow most foreign news or even complex domestic stories

Like reading novels + nonfiction © people like me!

Obsessive checking of email at work while in the midst of ~▓▓▓▓▓▓~

Laziness - sought out Reeeally easy job w/ downtime - BUT this ofte 5 years of hyperproductivity and

Can't sleep through night w/ bad habit

Gasp! Obsessive checking of email at work! —S.C.

(The "Bad Habits" continue on p. 239)

1. Favorite family memories 2. Least Favorite Family Memories
3. Reasons to start a family
4. Reasons Not to start a Family
5. Absurd Fights I've had with Siblings 6. Family conflicts 7. Things I should ask my mother/father about 8. Things I should do for a family member. 9. Why I love my parents 10. Friends who have been like family to me 11. Ways to show my friends I care about them
12. Reasons my parents were hypocrites 13. Parenting Lessons
14. Parenting Principles. 15. Wierd family rituals 16. Family food traditions 17. Names for imaginary children 18. Favorite grandparent memories 19. Geneology 20. Things I want my spouse to "honey do"

10 FAMILY and FRIENDS

Could a family function without lists? Look inside almost any suburban kitchen, and you'll find a list under a magnet on the refrigerator, or maybe even a special to-do list notepad with graphics on it. Baby names, home-improvement projects, grocery lists, doctors' appointments, Santa wish lists, and so on. The list goes on. The lists in this chapter are part of that blur, but they're a bit more unexpected. They are not so much "get milk" or "sign report card" as they are about how family members communicate with each other through lists.

Some are pure sweetness. Winter Fedyk's father asked her to write a list of things she likes about herself for his birthday. He then scanned it and sent it back to her. Some are remembered advice—"Things Mum Taught Me" (always take the milk from the back). "Things to do before getting pregnant" is one of my favorites because it expresses the ambivalence many women feel about the sacrifices they make to become mothers.

Other family lists are more about power struggles. Witness the "honey do" list phenomenon—that to-do list of household chores written by a wife for her husband. Millions of notepads are sold with "Honey Do" at the top, bumblebees and dripping pots of honey in the margins, the graphics designed to soften the blow—because let's face it: writing someone else a to-do list essentially amounts to bossing them around. In this chapter, "honey do" gets a new twist, when a twenty-eight-year-old daughter writes her fifty-two-year-old artist mother an extensive to-do list in an attempt to transform her into a more organized, morning person. She *tries* to soften the bossiness with a gigantic "I LOVE YOU!!"

Because friends are increasingly the new family, the people we confide in and see on a regular basis, I've also included lists by friends for friends. Well-known chef Alice Waters writes a list of ingredients for a friend's birthday dinner and *Village Voice* columnist Michael Musto keeps a list of movies to watch for his "Bad Movie Club." His list is so long you could certainly use it to start your own.

who: **JENNIFER COLVIN**

age: **ALMOST 30**

date: **MARCH 2006**

where: **DOWNTOWN OAKLAND, at work**

Almost Ready for Children

"I wanted to get married years before my husband did. I was desperate for security and wanted to start my real, grown-up life. Once we got married, we moved to the San Francisco Bay Area and started new lives. We started a marketing consulting business, bought a house, got a new group of friends, started grad school. I got all of the love and happiness and security I wanted, and everything was going so well, I didn't want to lose it all, to put everything aside to get pregnant. Then, problem was, as soon as we got married, my husband made a commitment to the whole shebang, including kids, and he didn't want to wait. I've been using my to-do list as an excuse for years, but at this point it's shorter (and more do-able) than it's ever been. It includes only the things I think I can accomplish in the next six months. At one time, there were a half-dozen countries on the list, and now there are just two. I guess that means I'm almost ready."

DIY LIST IDEA:
Things to Do Before Having Kids/
When My Children Are Grown

Before getting pregnant:

1. visit the people I know who live in other countries (Australia, Germany)
2. go whitewater rafting
3. finish one more semester of grad school
4. paint the front bedroom
5. drink lots of wine for my 30th b-day
6. ~~pay off credit cards~~
   sell crap on eBay (old PDA, snowboard, unwanted gifts)
7. do situps (3 x week)
8. take vitamins (every day)
9. ~~look at~~ read baby books my friends gave me

She forgot one thing: discontinue birth control. —S.C.

who: **STEPHANIE PATTERSON**

age: **28**

for: **HER MOTHER, SUSAN FELDKAMP, 52**

date: **MAY 2006**

where: **MESA, ARIZONA**

*a daughter's to-do list
for her mother*

"My daughter made this list because she thinks I should be more organized. I'm a graphic artist and work freelance after many years of working for someone else. Often I work whenever the mood strikes me, even if it is 1 or 2 a.m.; this drives my daughter a little nuts. I'm also a bead artist and spend many hours making necklaces, bracelets, and objects de art. I get absorbed and lose track of time, and organization has not been my strong suit. I hate to clean, and my daughter wants me to manage things better and be more of a morning person, so she made me this list to help me organize my time. Do I really need to be reminded to brush my teeth? No, she just threw that in for good measure. I don't need a reminder about taking a shower, either. My therapist thinks my daughter is young and needs to be more understanding of her old mother. Have I followed it? No. I get a giggle out of the list because my daughter isn't the most organized, either. She can't help it—she is related to me!"

DIY LIST IDEA:
Advice to Give My Mother

SUNDAY	REST ☺ Watch Charles Stanley @5pm (at home or @ Kathy's?)
MONDAY	LAUNDRY (BIG STUFF) TOWELS/SHEETS
TUESDAY	KITCHEN
WEDNESDAY	LIVING ROOM
THURSDAY	OFFICE
FRIDAY	BATHROOMS TOILETS WIPE DOWN COUNTERS/SINKS TRASH!!!! TAKE OUT!!! ☺
SATURDAY	LAUNDRY (clothes) Bedroom

I ♥ YOU!! ☺

Every day something new—......!
wake up at (eight) and ¡shower!.....!
Houswork from 8:30-10
(Don't forget breakfast! and
    brush your teeth!)
Skateland 10-12
lunch from 12-12:30 (or one!)
work again 1-5 (jeopardy in
    the background!)
deliveries 5-5:45
home by 6 to bead, (and dinner!)
IN BED BY MIDNIGHT!!! ✪

At least Stephanie's flexible about lunch. —S.C.

who: **CAROL CHALOUPKA**

age: **IN HER TEENS**

date: **SOMETIME IN THE 1950s**

discovered by: **HER DAUGHTER Maija Merchant**

remembering my
MOTHER

"My mom took five years to die from early onset Alzheimer's. My dad and I took care of her in our house in Sherman Oaks, California. She was in a wheelchair and needed help eating, bathing, and going to the bathroom. We moved her into a small private nursing home when I couldn't lift her anymore. I spent about thirty hours a week there. I would feed her and play music and sing to her. She didn't talk anymore but would smile and make funny faces sometimes, like fish lips and whatnot. Mostly she would just stare out the window. I held her hand when she passed away on May 9, 2005, the day after Mother's Day, and it was peaceful and we were all so relieved.

"When I wasn't with her I spent hours digging through dusty boxes of old photos, letters, report cards, postcards, medical records, wedding announcements, etc. My favorite find was this list my mother wrote at some point before she married my father in 1962. She was born in 1940, so she must have written it in high school or junior college. My mom did use sayings like these with us growing up. She was a very sweet, chipper person and tried to be positive in every situation. For example, instead of scolding me (I was a mouthy kid), she would use the 'before you say something' saying. I found the list long after she had lost the ability to talk. It's a treasure that's now fifty years old. It's the kind of thing I would run back into a burning house to save."

DIY LIST IDEA:
Sayings to Live By

CAROL CHALOUPKA

"Sayings To Live By"

1. The highest towers begin from the ground.

2. Thank God every morning when you get up that you have something to do that day whether you like it or not.

3. Be not merely good, be good for something.
                                    —Thoreau

4. Doing an injury puts you below your enemy; revenging one makes you but even with him; forgiving it sets you above him.
                            — Benjamin Franklin

5. "No man has a good enough memory to become a successful liar."
                                    —Lincoln

6. The difference between the possible and the impossible is — "The measure of man's will."
                            — Chinese Proverb

7. Confuses says, "A mind is like a parachute, it functions only when open!"

8. I yam what I yam!

9. Before you say something — ask yourself if it passes these three tests — 1. Is it True? 2. Is it Kind?, and, 3. Is it Necessary?

After a mother dies, her words live on. —S.C.

who: **LIL CAMERON**

age: **19**

date: **JANUARY 2006**

where: **AUCKLAND, NEW ZEALAND**

Mom's Advice

"My mother has taught me so many little tips for life, but I never remember them until I use one. So I started writing them down. I haven't gotten very far yet."

DIY LIST IDEA:
Advice from My Parents That I
Actually Follow

hings mum taught me:
- Take the milk from the back - the expiry date will be later
If a job's worth doing, it's worth doing well
There's nothing more attractive than a girl that's shitfaced.
Touch white when you see an ambulance (so you'll never be in one)

Do *you* take the milk from the back? —*S.C.*

A BIRTHDAY PRESENT
FOR DAD

"I wrote this list of things I like about myself, as part of the birthday card I gave to my dad one year. He asked me to do it, and I kept putting it off, and then finally he bugged me so much about it that I included it in his card. He then scanned it and sent it to me. He's in AA and I think this must be one of the exercises they do. It's hard to list the things you like about yourself. Especially when you think people might criticize you for it. Like the dude who made fun of me on your website for writing 'independant' instead of 'independent.' But whatever, I will never misspell that again!"

DIY LIST IDEA:
Ten Things I Like About Myself

· October 25th, 2001 ·

Happy birthday, Dad!

10 Things I Like About Me:
     (updated version © 2001)

1. I am independant and (mostly) responsible.
2. I have a University degree.
3. I have always tried to be nice to everyone regardless of race, class, etc. Because of this, people from highschool come up to me to say hi, even if I don't recognize them.
4. I have a good sense of humor.
5. I have (some) vision and direction for my life...
6. ... but I can roll with the punches, if need be.
7. I'm getting old enough now that I don't care if I don't look cool because I'm wearing a ski suit in winter in public.
8. ... but I'm still cool!
9. I have a good relationship with my family, and have learned to appreciate them.
10. I look forward to my life, and the challenges and opportunities before me. ↑Thank-you for helping me to be this person. I ♡ u Dad   winter

Who says wearing a ski suit in public isn't cool? —S.C.

who: **RACHEL LEDDY**

age: **7**

date: **1993**

where: **CHARLESTON, ILLINOIS**

list saved by: **HER FATHER, MICHAEL**

Supplies For an Imaginary CAMPING TRIP

"I've had this list on the wall in my office for years. My daughter Rachel wrote it for an imaginary camping trip. It's a beautiful moment from kidhood—so serious, so careful (the really painstaking cursive writing), and so fanciful. As to why I've saved it, it's by one of my kids. Save everything!"

DIY LIST IDEA:
Most Important Childhood Friends
(Imaginary and Otherwise)

Flashlight

Food

shoe

bananas

blue crayon

thats all

who: **PATRICIO PINTO**

age: **39**

date: **MAY 2005**

where: **BARCELONA**

Emily Songs

"This is the list of tracks of a CD that I burned for my only niece, Emilia, who is six years old. I live in Barcelona, and my niece lives in Santiago, Chile, with her parents, one of whom is my brother. So this is in some way a means of keeping in touch with her, making her feel that she is on my mind, and a way of making her get familiar with different types of music, so she can develop her own tastes in the future. She really liked the CD. She kept it in the player beside her bed so she could listen to it before going to sleep."

DIY LIST IDEA:
Mix Tape for Someone I Love

0326 Bad / 0348 Cal / 0325 Seb

tipos 3
tipos 6.

0120 viv

Emilia — Silvio Rodriguez
Emily — Adam Green
Emily — Manic Street Preachers
For Emily, Whenever i may find Her — Simon and Garfunkel
When Emily cries — Television Personalities
Emily, Sing something sweet to me — Bright Eyes
Emily — Ween
Emily — Keane
A Rose for Emily — Zombies
See Emily Play — Pink Floyd
~~Fets Parids — Emily~~

↳ "Mix-Tape para mi sobrina
Emilia".

Bayer
- acabados
- cotas interiores
- alturas interiores
- muros interiores
- Falso techo
- zerizos medidas armarios.

Who knew there were so many Emily songs? —S.C.

who: **CHEF ALICE WATERS**

when: **CIRCA 2003**

where: **BERKELEY, CALIFORNIA**

list interpreted by: **SYLVAN BRACKETT,**
 Alice's assistant

Alice Waters Cooks for a Friend

"This list is the beginning of a menu that Alice assembled for a small dinner party she threw for her friend Sue's birthday. It was just the beginning of asparagus season and she was thinking of ways to use asparagus. The crossed-out bit on the bottom was 'Dalai Lama pasta'—a pasta dish we cooked when the Dalai Lama visited our restaurant, Chez Panisse. She didn't make the Dalai Lama pasta because it didn't contain asparagus."

DIY LIST IDEA:
What I Want for My Birthday Dinner

porkchops
beans.
kale.

salad
crêpes

asparagus salad
eggs bacon.

chicken mutton white asparagus
potatoes / rissotto

Sue's BD

artichoke
pasta
parmesan

onions
garlic
rice
beans
anchovies
parmesan
fennel.
polion
Chronicle

Ahh, to have Alice Waters cook your birthday dinner. —*S.C.*

who: *VILLAGE VOICE* COLUMNIST
MICHAEL MUSTO

when: 2002–PRESENT

where: IN HIS "LUXURIOUS" NYC APARTMENT

terrible MOVIES IN *enjoyable* COMPANY

"This is the lineup for my Bad Movie Club—four friends and I who regularly meet in my apartment to watch movies that should have been good but weren't. Next to each title, I generally put the store that carries it (Kim's, TLA, Tower) or I write 'Dennis,' meaning our film critic friend Dennis Dermody has a copy. Once we've seen the film, I cross it out. It's an ongoing, evolving list, which I started about five years ago when I realized there are so many bad movies out there that I had to catalog the best of the worst. The club is sick, ritualistic, and much more fun than watching a good movie."

DIY LIST IDEA:
Five Best Bad Movies Ever

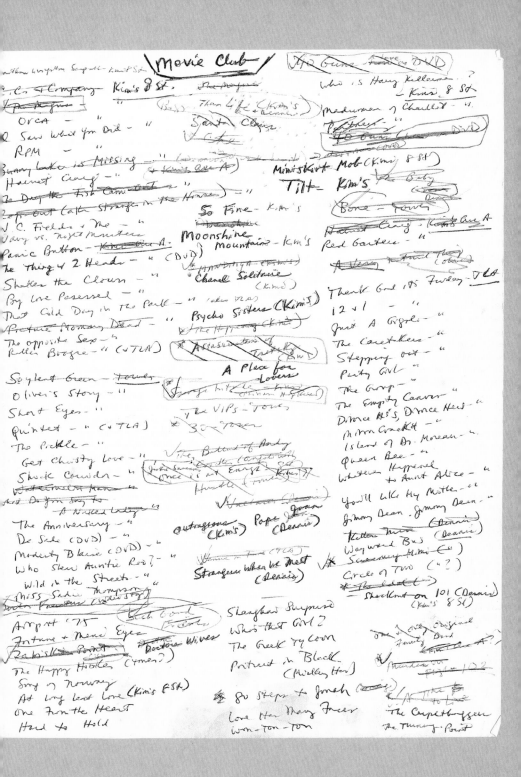

Start your own bad movie club with this list. —*S.C.*

"Gratitude is not only the greatest of virtues, but the parent of all others."

— Cicero

11 happiness and hates

Happiness lists are among my favorites to read. When I read them, pleasure suddenly seems so available, so not necessarily tied to the perfect job, mate, or pair of jeans. In a way, I think of these happiness lists as a rebuttal to consumer culture. I don't need to buy anything new, I just need to notice details like "sunshine" or "having the house to myself" and focus on them by writing them down.

Writing happiness lists can also be therapeutic. If I have trouble sleeping, I write lists of good things that happened that day before bed: a noon call from a boyfriend to say hello, catching my reflection in the mirror at the gym and actually liking it. My happiness lists soothe my brain into thinking everything is okay rather than roving for the next problem to solve. Though I never read it, my nightly lists were probably semi-inspired by the bestselling book *Simple Abundance,* which advocates writing gratitude lists. The idea: Write five things a day for which you are grateful, and observe increased feelings of peace over time. Does it work? Maybe. I find it hard to stay on a gratitude list regimen because sometimes writing one seems forced and Pollyanna-ish.

Happiness lists can have their dark side, too. There can be an undercurrent of sadness in them, an attempt to mask conditions that are not so great or to will ourselves into a better state. The woman who wrote "Ten Reasons to Be Happy" finds it amusing that she included "God." "I was probably reaching to get to number ten," she said. "I wasn't that happy."

So what does make us happy? There's not a single luxury item on these lists. They're not about major life milestones like marriage or home ownership, either. They're about small daily details. Recurring themes include rain, a sky full of stars, friends (old and new), the feeling of fresh-cut grass, sushi, going to the movies alone, confidence, and brown-paper packages tied up with string (which must have been plucked from Rodgers and Hammerstein's "My Favorite Things").

There's pleasure in anticipation, too, so this chapter also includes lists of planned happiness: "Foods I'll Eat Soon" and "Places to See Before I Die." For contrast, I also included lists of hates. I wouldn't advocate writing lists of hates before bed, but there can be an affirming power in pinpointing that which we despise.

who: **A WOMAN IN HER LATE TWENTIES**

date: **1999**

where: **IN HER BEDROOM**

Reaching for *Happiness*

"I make these ten-reasons-to-be-happy lists constantly. I probably made one in the last week. This was eight years ago. I look
back and think, Who was Ken? He wasn't that nice. 'I have a
great computer'—I feel like in this particular list I was kind of
stretching. I wasn't that happy. You notice how I put 'God'—I
don't normally put God on the list. When you make these lists
it's an attempt to look on the bright side, but sometimes when
you look back at them they are slightly pathetic. [Laughs.]
Yeah, I did have great roommates."

DIY LIST IDEA:
Ten Reasons to Be Happy Today

10 Reasons to be happy

1. I am healthy.
2. I am writing a novel.
3. I can pay my bills this month.
4. I have great roomates.
5. Ken is nice and cute.
6. I have a great computer.
7. I can bisit my parents soon.
8. God
9. I feel attractive.
10. I have written wonderful poets

who: **A RECENT COLLEGE GRADUATE**

age: **22**

date: **2002**

where: **LOS ANGELES, at a food court in the Koreatown Galleria**

What Works for Me

"Why is swimming in rivers and lakes a reason to live? That's just something I love. I can't tell you why. I'm always the first to jump in."

DIY LIST IDEA:
My Reasons for Living

Reasons for Living

Trader Joes
plastic big feet
art that you stumble upon
KCRW
Wilco's "she's a jar"
reading there's mind — weird ESP moment btn. us
finding something unique
events
vegetarian sushi
parents that really care abt. me
Mission District Murals
drawing/doodling
getting praise
Bob Dylan
kereoke
going to movies alone
people sometimes find me funny/smart
taking photographs
friends I really like
Lucinda Williams
Adam + Emma
swimming in rivers/lakes
cooking
tofu
Stephen Malkmus
cameron crowe
Ikea
Halo
Sasha
Mochi
street festivals

I love this list, but maybe Trader Joe's shouldn't be her number one reason for living. —S.C.

who: **JENNIFER STAAB**

age: **30**

date: **AUGUST 2004**

where: **BIEL, SWITZERLAND**

Dried Tears on Cheeks

"I was helping start a small school and going through the growing pains of entering my thirties while also getting ready to leave after living in Switzerland for a year. I wanted to somehow capture some of what living there meant to me. I think that making a list of favorite things pushes me to commit to them. To say, Yes, these *are* my favorites. Other to-do lists are more goal-oriented. This list was more about commitment and memory. Why 'dried tears on cheeks'? I like seeing the mark of tears on people. Tears are a very private thing, but when people just let the tears fall off their face without wiping them away, it's like they let you in on their pain."

DIY LIST IDEA:
My Favorite Things

20.08.01   two weeks from today and we go home.

<u>Favorite things</u>
new box of crayons
walking barefoot after Rain.
~~Kneel~~
smell of fresh baked bread
discovering a ~~good~~ poetry book.

~~Sitting around a table w/~~
~~friends~~
a table full of empty, half-empty
wine & water glasses.

Large, drooping roses,
    petals falling ~~to the flo~~

~~Mail in the~~
mail with overseas postage

bear hugs

~~Swinging high~~ underdog pushes on swings

~~Laund~~ ~~hanging wet~~ ~~laundry; hanging &~~
~~blowing~~
~~wind blowing the hanging laund~~
hanging laundry drying in the sun

the pattern of dried tears on cheeks

who: **MELISSA MORRISON**

when: **SOON AFTER GRADUATING FROM COLLEGE**

date: **1989**

where: **DALLAS**

"All these things, in their own way, still comprise my ideal world. Being confident, acting like myself with a boyfriend. Others were about career, and others about money, namely having a car I could trust. (The car I was driving had recently broken down outside Texarkana.) Now I'm at a point where I don't really have to worry about whether my car's going to make it, yet I'm still aware of what a relief it is to have that kind of security. I managed to get two brief articles published in *Rolling Stone*—not quite the career there I had envisioned—but I basically accomplished everything else on the list. The thing about a list is, when it's on the page, you pretty much have to get it done. Otherwise the list just stares you down."

DIY LIST IDEA:
Ten Things That Define My Ideal World

An Ideal World

Read the New York Times every
    morning.
Write for Rolling Stone
Come up with good story ideas
Have a car I can trust
Be myself with boyfriends
Be unwaveringly confident
Have long hair
Remember things I read
Think deeper
Transcend the limits

Is there really such a thing as unwavering confidence? —S.C.

who: **A WOMAN IN HER EARLY THIRTIES**

date: **PROBABLY CIRCA 2005**

where: **IN HER LIVING ROOM**

simple truths

(but no people)

"I make lots of lists of why I should be grateful. Then I make lists of more immediate pleasures. It's not a grand list, but at this moment, am I okay? It's almost like checking out that my most important immediate needs are being met."

DIY LIST IDEA:
My Most Immediate Needs: Are They Being Met?

*

*

*

5 happiness

1 no work

2 book

3 sleep

4 food

5 money

Did this start out as a game of hangman? —*S.C.*

who: **MEGHAN BURCH**

age: **25 (added last line at 26)**

dates: **MAY 2005 AND JULY 2006**

where: **CHICOPEE, MASSACHUSETTS**

Thanking God

"I don't often write gratitude lists to God, but I do occasionally write prayers so that I can make them concrete—take time with them, instead of rushing through them in my head. Reading back on this list, it sounds as though I wanted to thank God for answered prayers. Judging by dates of other writings in the notebook, it was around the time some difficult situations at work were resolved. He had taught me a lot in that time. The line about surfing I added after a great day at the beach. Friends of ours took us to Rhode Island and taught us how to use the board. I didn't think I would like it, but on my first wave, I was standing. It was amazing! I never thought I could do that. I bailed on some rocks after that first wave, but was proud to bear the bruise."

DIY LIST IDEA:
Things I'm Grateful For

Dear God,

A list of things I am grateful for today:
- Jesus' calling us to life in him.
- My loving husband and his role in bringing me to Jesus
- Providing me not only with a means to pay bills, but an opportunity to learn. I know that you are constantly preparing & shaping me for what you have in store for me.
- For your answering my plea for relief from how my job used to be. You have blessed me!
- Thank you for using me - I pray that I am bringing glory to you. Help me show you are the source of my strength.
- Your faithfulness & love
- Better digestion today
- Your helping me resist buying things I know I don't need. That will always be a struggle.
- A place to live, a bed to sleep in
- Tomorrow's breakfast, lunch & dinner already in the kitchen cabinets.
- For ideas that help me do my job well.
- A car that gets me where I need to go
- For patience with me and provision of comfort even when I neglect spending time in prayer with you.
- Surfing and eating fruit salad at the beach.

Better digestion today, surfing and fruit salad at the beach tomorrow. —S.C.

who: **A YOUNG WOMAN**

age: **19**

date: **AUGUST 2005**

where: **AUCKLAND, NEW ZEALAND**

"Sometimes when I'm out and about I see things that make me feel happy about life. I wrote this list because I wanted to remember them. I don't want to forget why it is great to be alive. I wrote the Pet Hates list because I saw a boy spit on the pavement in front of me one day and thought, How disgusting. Also because whenever you try to think of your pet hates you can never remember them. (Well, I can't.)"

DIY LIST IDEA:
Pet Loves/Pet Hates

Things I like:
The smell of fresh-cut grass, & sudden rain on a hot pavement
Young dads with their kids
People smiling to themselves at a memory or thought
Making lists
Going to the movies or dinner alone
Going to cafe alone & reading
Getting my head massaged at the hairdressers
Asian girls holding hands
Sharp pencils
Girls sharing earphones
The smell of freshly roasted coffee beans
Old friends
A clean house
The excitement of meeting someone new
that you really like
Having the house to myself

Pet hates/dislikes
Boys spitting on the pavement
Bad punctuation & spelling - especially if it
is intentional & on their online dating profiles
When people cut their nails inside & say they
are going to catch all the pieces
Cheap people (as in tightarses)
When Matthias purposefully patronizes me when
he says "Li-lly" in that tone
Drink driving
People romantically feeding each other

Not a typo: "Drink driving" is the term for "drunk driving" in New Zealand. —S.C.

who: **AN EARLY-TWENTIES WOMAN**

when: **CIRCA 2003**

where: **SOUTHERN CALIFORNIA**

Getting The Shit Out

"This list was basically about getting the shit out of my head. After I wrote this I went to a playwriting workshop where the leader had the whole class take five minutes at the beginning to write down all the bullshit in their heads, just to get all the crap out so they could write the good stuff. I think that's more or less what I was trying to do here."

DIY LIST IDEA:
Thoughts to Remove from My Head

things that I hate:

Glenda
smog
logistics — making plans, not making plans, people
 breaking plans
being a virgin — never having any want no/
 find me attractive
constant anxiety that there's something
 fundamental / life changing / important
 that I should be doing instead
George Bush — so many injustices & horrible
 state of the world, impossible to list
Grey Davis
having to pay attention to details
sitting in the office all day
feeling a huge disconnect w/ my brother
lying to my parents
having such high rent
living alone, but I hate bad roommates more
that I'm fat
wishing I was truly, identifiably talented
 at something
that I don't live in Seattle in the early
 70s (a la singles)
that I'm not Cameron Crowe
that I'm so damn messy
getting in fights
that I had such an unhappy junior
 high / high school experience + no
 friends from that period

Aren't you glad you aren't twenty-two anymore? —S.C.

who: **REBECCA STEVENS**

age: **21**

date: **CIRCA 1996**

Cheesy and Delicious

"I wrote this list during the tail end of a three-month road trip with my then-boyfriend. I was twenty-one then, thirty-one now. We were camping and eating well, but a homegirl has cravings. I am a pastry chef and sous chef now, but when I wrote the list I had just worked at posh cafés and would soon start baking professionally. I probably ate all those things, definitely by now, and many of them by myself. Apparently it's rare, but I think nothing of making something nice just for myself. Foods I'll eat soon, now? Tough question. I think my plum crostada is off the hook, so I plan on eating that soon."

DIY LIST IDEA:
Foods I Want to Try

▷ FOODS I'LL EAT SOON ◁

- herb salad ~ honey/lemon
- curried carrot soup w. coconut milk
- penne w. aubergines, fresh tomatoes, basil, riotta, and parmesan
- miso soups w. vegetables
- swiss chard
- sandwiches for my breaks at work
- fritata potato, zuccini
- mixed vegetables w. ginger
- cheese melts w. whole wheat bread ᵗᵛᵉᵍ
- braised fennel w. lemon sauce
- saffron rice w. tomatoes and peas
- gnocchi w. tomato ~rose~ sauce, green beans, basil and parmesan
- spinach w. sesame seeds + red peppers
- brocoli w. cheddar miso sauce
- bocoli w. onions garlic + w. roux broth sauce over rice
- hicous salads w. toast shallot dressing
- plantains w. black beans·rice
- sesame seed crusted tofu or fig+mash taco style ᵗᵛᵉᵍ ᵖᵒʳᵏ
- stuffed bell peppers
- cheese choices, greens everyday

Yum. —S.C.

who: **JUDY WESTPHAL**

date: **1989 (but list has been recopied many times)**

where: **DE PERE, WISCONSIN**

WORLD TRAVEL

"I started writing the list in 1989 when I was a high school senior. I went to school in a small town and always dreamed of seeing the world. Since then I have had to recopy it because it was folded and refolded many times. The crossed-off places mean I have been there and done that. I like traveling alone and meeting up with friends and family at certain places. On average I take about two trips every year. I try to go to at least one new destination. Crossing things off gives me a great sense of making my mark in the world."

DIY LIST IDEA:
Places to See Before I Die

Places I want to visit before I die
<u>France</u>

    * Paris — Eiffel Tower, Louvre, Notre Dame

    * French Riviera — go topless on a beach
                 in the Mediterranean

<u>Italy</u>

    * Rome

    * Venice — go on a Gondola ride

    * Vatican City — see the Vatican

    * Florence — see statue of David

    * Pisa — see the Leaning Tower of Pisa

<u>England</u>

    * London — see Stonehedge

    * Bath

    * Dover — see white cliffs of Dover

<u>Germany</u>

<u>Holland</u>

    * Amsterdam — see Ann Frank's house
          & red light district
        (especially a coffee house)

<u>Austria</u>

<u>Belgium</u>

<u>Denmark</u>

<u>Liechtenstein</u>

<u>Switzerland</u> — see the Swiss Alps

<u>Mexico</u>

<u>Monaco</u>

<u>Ireland</u>

<u>Jamaica</u>

Luckily this is just page one. We don't want Judy to die after Ireland. —*S.C.*

who: **EMILY MUNRO**

age: **7**

date: **WINTER 2007**

where: **LITTLETON, COLORADO**

a PERFECT
afternoon

"What do I like writing lists about? Everything. I like adding to my mom's shopping lists. Once I added 'marshmallows.' She wouldn't buy them if they weren't on her list. I wrote a list of things we wanted to do with my grandma."

DIY LIST IDEA:
Things I Used to Like to Do with
My Grandmother

What I want to
do with grandma

Make Cokies
Watch movies
have hot chocolate
Play bord games

"Why do women like making lists?"

"Women don't like making lists."

"Yes, they do. They're never quite so happy as when they're making themselves a little list. Did you ever think about why you make lists?"

"It's so I can cross things off. Did you ever think about why you've got so much crap in your wallet?"

—Dialogue from _Sports Night_, Aaron Sorkin's late-nineti sitcom about a fictional sports-news show and the people who work on it

APPENDIX

OUR LISTS, OURSELVES: TODOLISTBLOG.COM SURVEY RESULTS ON THE LIST-MAKING NATION

Our fellow list-makers are all around us, but how much do we really know about their habits and quirks, and how our own styles compare? There have been no major studies commissioned by universities or the government. To fill the gap, I took a survey on todolistblog.com in August 2006. About six hundred people responded. Complete findings are below.

1. WHO MAKES MORE LISTS: MEN OR WOMEN?

84% Female

16% Male

Women are the dominant list sex. You would think that everyone would make lists in equal numbers—men and women alike. Why not? We all need them to get things done. But in this survey, 84 percent of respondents were women. Why so many more women listers than men? Maybe it's about humility. Just as men stereotypically don't like to ask for directions, maybe a lot of men don't want to admit they might need the direction of lists. Maybe it's because women are still the world's multitaskers, expected to bring home the bacon and take responsibility for the home. Maybe it's because women just like lists! To be clear, men do write lists, too! Every man I've dated recently wants to show me his.

2. WHAT DO WE PREFER: WRITING LISTS WITH PEN AND PAPER OR ON THE COMPUTER?

89% Prefer pen and paper

11% Prefer writing lists electronically

Pen and paper still wins. Dozens of to-do-list software programs promise to help us organize our lives online and in PDAs, and a growing number of people are taking advantage. But there's more to list making than productivity and organization. Sometimes it's about preserving dysfunction, writing on any available surface: a magazine subscription card, the margin of a newspaper, a credit-card offer! It's often about the pleasure of doing something that's *not* on the computer, embracing the tactile pleasures of putting pen to paper, doodling, taking a meditative moment. People often said they feel more accountable to their daily lists when they're written in their own handwriting.

3. DO WE ENJOY MAKING LISTS?

89% Enjoy making lists

11% Don't enjoy making lists

Yes, but . . . the vast majority says they enjoy making lists, but for others, "enjoyable" might be too strong a word. For them, writing lists is more a matter of daily survival—they wouldn't know how to function without them.

4. HOW DO WE ACKNOWLEDGE OURSELVES FOR COMPLETING A TASK?

66% cross tasks off

21% write a check mark next to it

5% do nothing (let it be)

4% write a check next to it

Crossing off is most common. Most people cross things off rather than making neat little check marks. Four percent make X marks. A full 5 percent do nothing. Perplexing: Isn't the whole point of writing lists to cross things off?

5. HOW MANY WRITE DOWN TASKS *AFTER* ACCOMPLISHING THEM, THEN CROSS THEM OFF?

50% Write down tasks after already doing them

50% That's bizarre

Many of us cheat. Surprise, surprise: This quirk is not so uncommon. A full 50 percent confessed to adding tasks after completing them, then gleefully crossing them off. This way, they have a more complete picture of everything they've done, plus the chance to cross something else off. (It's sort of insane how much we love crossing things off, isn't it?) Sometimes assigning an easy task like "write to-do list" is a strategic move. A completely new list can be daunting. But once we start, we have to keep going.

6. DO WE SPEND MORE TIME MAKING LISTS OR MORE TIME DOING THINGS ON THEM?

77% Spend more time accomplishing things on them

23% Spend more time making lists

7. DO LISTS MAKE US MORE PRODUCTIVE?

86% Lists help make me more productive

14% My lists are a procrastination tool

Making lists can be time-consuming. Almost a quarter of us spend more time perfecting lists than doing anything on them. But oddly, in a follow-up question, only 14 percent said their lists are a procrastination tool.

8. DO YOU WRITE LISTS IN CODE?

71% I have never written a list in code

29% I've written a list in code

Almost a third of us have written lists in code. Ever written a list in code so that other people would not be able to read it? Twenty-nine percent of respondents were this crafty and beguiling. Most common code: for women to write "tampons," "birth control," or "maxi pads" in code (T, BC, or MP) on shopping lists, often because they were at work and didn't want the boss or coworkers to walk by and see they were buying feminine hygiene products. A gay man told me about coded lists he kept as a teenager. "Sx" meant sex, "trees" meant pot, and "ex" meant exercise. "No brm" meant "Don't go to the public bathrooms and have sex with men."

9. IS LIFE BETTER OR WORSE BECAUSE OF TO-DO LISTS?

96% Say life is better with to-do lists

4% Say life is worse with to-do lists

We're better off with lists than without them. The overwhelming majority of respondents said life is better because of lists. They're more organized, less stressed, and more productive. Some respondents said life was half better, half worse. Without lists, they would be in a constant state of panic, but if they let go of their to-do lists, they might be more able to live in the moment.

10. DO YOU EVER MAKE TO-DON'T LISTS?

74% I've never made a to-don't list

26% I've made a to-don't list

A quarter of us have made to-don't lists. Most common theme: kinds of men not to date or sleep with.

11. DO LISTS IMPROVE OUR LOVE LIVES?

51% Have made a list describing their ideal mate

49% Have not

Opinion is split. Just over half of respondents have made a list describing their dream mate, but only 38 percent think such a list is helpful in terms of finding or evaluating a potential partner. We love writing dream-date lists when we're alone; we also recognize they can limit our vision for acceptable mates. Once we meet someone and feel an actual connection, the list is often forgotten. A list can only go so far in anticipating the unique connection between two human beings.

12. HOW COMMON IS IT TO ITEMIZE OUR SEXUAL PAST?

55% Have not!

45% Have made lists of people they've slept with

What's your number? Almost half of respondents are keeping track of theirs.

13. HOW WIDESPREAD IS LIST OBSESSION (GLAZOMANIA)?

72% No, I'm not!

28% Yes, I'm an obsessive list-maker

What makes a true list-maker obsessive? Respondents say they know they are when: they're making lists multiple times a day and *always* recopying by hand to make them neater; they can't continue if the title isn't right; they can't go to the bathroom without putting it on the list; and they're not ironically detached from the contents of their lists.

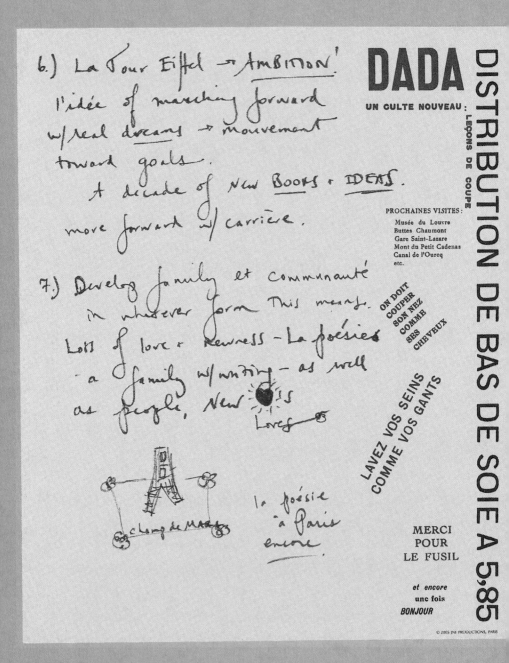

ANNUAL BIRTHDAY LIST Continued from p. 33

want it

7) I will gossip a little less maliciously with Ruth.

8) I will not eat as much.

9) I will not fall into bed without brushing my hair & teeth, no matter what time it is.

10) I will always walk with my head up, and not wiggle so much.

11) I will not pay for dates with kisses.

12) I will not go out with icky boys, ever!

Continued from p. 53

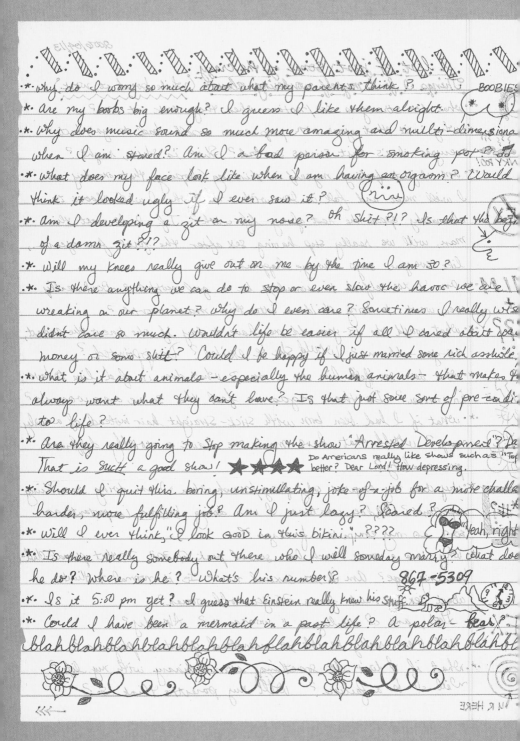

-*- why do I worry so much about what my parents think?

-*- Are my boobs big enough? I guess I like them alright. BOOBIES

-*- Why does music sound so much more amazing and multi-dimensional when I am stoned? Am I a bad person for smoking pot?

-*- What does my face look like when I am having an orgasm? Would I think it looked ugly if I ever saw it?

-*- Am I developing a zit on my nose? Oh shit?!? Is that the beginning of a damn zit?!?

-*- Will my knees really give out on me by the time I am 30?

-*- Is there anything we can do to stop or even slow the havoc we are wreaking on our planet? Why do I even care? Sometimes I really wish I didn't care so much. Wouldn't life be easier if all I cared about was money or some shit? Could I be happy if I just married some rich asshole?

-*- What is it about animals - especially the human animals - that makes us always want what they don't have? Is that just some sort of pre-condition to life?

-*- Are they really going to stop making the show "Arrested Development"? Do Americans really like shows such as "Top Model" better? Dear Lord! How depressing. That is such a good show! ★★★★

-*- Should I quit this boring, unstimulating, joke-of-a-job for a more challenging, harder, more fulfilling job? Am I just lazy? Scared? Shit!

-*- Will I ever think, "I look good in this bikini." ???? "yeah, right"

-*- Is there really somebody out there who I will someday marry? What does he do? Where is he? What's his number? 867-5309

-*- Is it 5:00 pm yet? I guess that Einstein really knew his stuff.

-*- Could I have been a mermaid in a past life? A polar bear?

blah blah blah blah blah blah flah blah blah blah blah blah bl

Bored at Work Continued from p. 71

cooking — no major fast food
cooks / appreciates / validates my cooking
yes
likes garlic

home habits — seat down on toilet

Not too anal, mello @ house, but clean

Not ego driven, confident in self

No snoring (sound sleeper)
cuddler

Mature enough — to discern when/what
— doesn't try in front of people

Fun & goofy w/ me — shopping, playing

open minded to all things

Career — passionate about his work
Maybe doing something physical
something I am interested in/can relate to/peeks my interest

Energy level — laid back
good communication skills
educated — interesting communication
eager to travel

Therapy / Healing → started, interested, wants to continue
— Spiritual

Collects Junk - lots of junk
starts things- doesn't finish them
feet twitch in sleep
Snores
eats badly-
Eats all of his meals - out
Bad relationship w/ father
Has Legal trouble
Has Bad Credit
has a Rural KS Accent
Uneducated Speech
Uneducated Thinking
Doesn't seem to like reading
Has a History of Violence (faults)
Very Hard to Hear orating
Bad Orater
Mumbles to himself all the time
Has a small mouth
Has a small tongue
Very seldom french Kisses
Can't breath very well most of the time
fearful alot
Allergic to Charlie
Bad taste in clothes & furnishings

Better off ALONE

Continued from p. 123

Tune out during office meetings
Spend too much money on lunch rather
    than bring a healthy lunch
Don't get up to meditate
Hireds omone to clean twice
Look at potential mates online
    in a superficial manner
Ego-driven - want to tell my
    story rather than others
Lazy at repating
~~Falling back~~ on supposed
    ADD [~~xxxxxx~~ ~~xxxxx~~ leave,
    which may be true
Never file - next move.
Hire org. consultant - a force
this self w/ B.'s help
Haven't started saving nestegg or
    retirement
Fall into mini-depressions about once or
    twice a month that last a few
    days - not terribly deep but
    hard hand must always remember
    a different chemical balance and
    ~~brighter~~ fews will come.

who: **SASHA CAGEN**

when: **NOVEMBER 4, 2006**

where: **CHOW RESTAURANT, SAN FRANCISCO**

list written down by: **ADAM DINGLE**

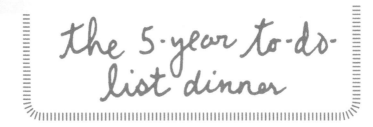

the 5-year to-do-list dinner

"One night my friends Sonya, Adam, and Kenneth and I were out at dinner before seeing a play, and Sonya came up with a brilliant to-do-list idea: We should write five-year to-do lists for one another—at least five things to accomplish by 2011. Her reasoning: If we wrote our own lists, we would be limited by our own imaginations. But if we gave one another aspirations, our lists (and lives) might take unexpected directions—and we would have the support of our friends to complete them.

"Sonya wanted to keep our lists in a special envelope and return them to us on November 4, 2011, but I stole mine back to use on this page. 'Write a horse?' was supposed to be 'Ride a horse,' but Adam didn't hear correctly (or he was being sarcastic and wanted to give me a creative challenge). Riding a horse is not really my deepest desire. In fact, I've already cantered. But who knows, maybe writing a horse will be more exciting. I'll have to find some way to do it over the next five years."

DIY LIST IDEA:
My Five-Year To-Do List
According to My Best Friend

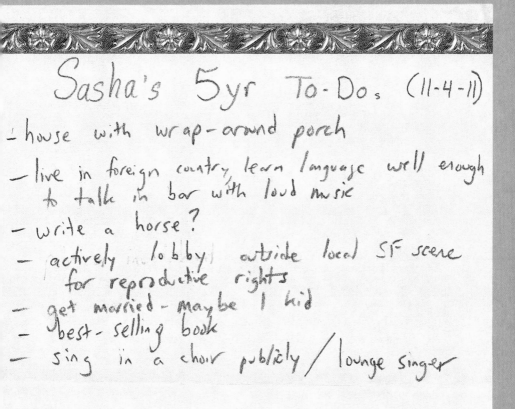

Sasha's 5yr To-Dos (11-4-11)

- house with wrap-around porch
- live in foreign country, learn language well enough to talk in bar with loud music
- write a horse?
- actively lobby outside local SF scene for reproductive rights
- get married - maybe 1 kid
- best-selling book
- sing in a choir publicly / lounge singer

Let's hope you're holding number 6 in your hands. —*S.C.*

Emily Fitzgerald

ABOUT THE AUTHOR

Sasha Cagen was born in Rhode Island and graduated from Barnard College. Her essays have appeared in *The Village Voice, Men's Health,* the *San Francisco Chronicle,* and in numerous anthologies. She was the founding editor of *To-Do List*, a print magazine that used the idea of a to-do list to explore details of modern life, and of todolistblog.com, a blog that publishes handwritten lists. She is also the author of *Quirkyalone: A Manifesto for Uncompromising Romantics,* a singles manifesto for a new generation, and is the force behind quirkyalone.net and International Quirkyalone Day, a growing alternative to Valentine's Day that celebrates all forms of love on February 14. She is currently at work on StyleMob, a new online community that aims to democratize fashion. Sasha Cagen lives in San Francisco where she writes lists on a daily basis, frequently writing down tasks that she has already accomplished so she can triumphantly cross them off.

Thank you for helping me create this book....

Acknowledgments!

Thank you for helping me create this book

Sara Cambridge!!!

Jill Grinberg (agent extraordinaire)

Jenny Bitner!!!

Amanda Patten   Sonya Worthy

Everyone who came to the 1st party! (Sonya, Kennedy, Adam, and many others)

Kenneth Wong
Cami Walker
Danielle Jatlow

Elline Lipkin

Liz Worthy and everyone else in writing group

Cameron Tuttle!!!

Flower
Michael
Nell ♥

Mike Chorost   Alex Tomisson   Christina Amini

Annie Millar!!!

Ellie
Everyone who worked on To-Do List magazine, esp. Burns Maxey!

OWEN CARLSEN

Ali Berzon! (that original for blog idea @ Mel's Diner)

Laura
Andrew
Sara S.
Hannah
Ed M.
Cristina
Spain ↳ Javier

Dad!   Bethany

Mom!   Dan...

Everyone who sent in lists!